Men Are Like A Pair of Shoes

A Single Woman's Guide to Choosing the Right Pair

First Edition

Jeff Carta

Two Ears Publishing
Lake Forest, California

Men Are Like a Pair of Shoes

A single woman's guide to choosing the right pair
by Jeff Carta

Published by:
Two Ears Publishing
P.O. Box 1300
Lake Forest, CA 92609

Order at www.menarelikeapairofshoes.com.

Copyright 2003 by Jeff Carta

ISBN, print edition: 0-9729242-4-8

Library of Congress Cataloging-in-Publication Data

Library of Congress Control Number: 2003091708

Carta, Jeff
Men Are Like a Pair of Shoes: A single woman's guide to choosing the right pair / by Jeff Carta. – 1st ed.
ISBN 0-9729242-4-8
Library of Congress Control Number: 2003091708
Printed in the United States of America

Men Are Like A Pair of Shoes

Jeff Carta

To my wife, Theresa,

*the woman who offered everything on
my list and even more*

Acknowledgments

Being a first-time author, I had an enormous amount of fun with this project. It has been challenging at times and rewarding at other points.

There have been many people who have been supportive of this project from the beginning. Most of all, I'd like to thank my wife Theresa, who has been my most vocal cheerleader. Her excitement about the book in the beginning helped boost my confidence to write it.

Robin Quinn, of Brainstorm Editorial, helped turn my thoughts and ideas into the book you are about to read. With utter professionalism and creativity, she helped transform my vision into reality. With Robin's experience and knowledge, our work relationship flowed smoothly. She was unafraid to take on this author's first work. She listened and always keeps the integrity of the book a priority. I thank Robin for exceeding my expectations.

Thanks to Chuck Casella, whose design of the book cover was inspired. Chuck's ability to be versatile and creative helped me feel comfortable. I knew a professional was handling the design of the project.

Appreciation also goes to Jenny Ricks, who drew the illustrations that captured the spirit of the book.

A special thanks to Jackie Casella for her last-minute proofreading skills. Your last-minute insights added much to the final edit.

Thank you to my parents Florence and Joe Carta, who showed support for this project from the very start.

Thank you to my in-laws, Ralph and Rosemary Jefferson, for all their prayers on my behalf.

Our children—Gina, Rachel, Carl, Joel, Philip and Rosemary—have blessed my life and Theresa's. The experiences my wife and I have had with them helped in the writing of this book.

A few friends and family members were there for me in very supportive ways and I want to acknowledge them especially. Tanya Needham, Emily Neumann and Bill Miller, each of you helped me in ways you may not know. Thank you!

To Robert Kiyosaki, author of *Rich Dad Poor Dad*. After hearing on your tape set "everyone has a million-dollar idea in his or her head and most do not get it out. I wrote this book. It is out now. Thank you for challenging me to write this book.

To Dan Poynter for writing your book Successful Nonfiction. Before I knew if I was going to write this book, I bought your book and its wisdom and insight made this whole process possible.

Last but not least, my thanks to God. Thank you for helping me find my way and follow my dreams.

Table of Contents

Table of Contents

About the Author

Years ago, author Jeff Carta used his own "Shopping List" to find Theresa—the woman he has been happily married to for 13 years. Jeff has lived and used the information in this book, and as he watched friends and his adult children go through the dating process, he decided to share his thoughts and perspectives on dating in a lighthearted way. The author opted to write a book for women, rather than men, because he believes that while men do the asking, women do the choosing..

When Jeff was chosen by his ideal mate Theresa, he not only put on the husband hat but also became an instant stepfather to Theresa's three children, Rachel , Carl , and Joel. In addition to his own daughter, Gina, Jeff became the sole father figure to Theresa's children. He took on the financial responsibility for them as well. Jeff did this gladly, because he knew that Theresa was his ideal mate. Theresa held all the qualities that he had been looking for. Jeff and Theresa went on to add two additional children to their family, with the births of their son Philip and then of their daughter Rosemary. It has not been an easy road but has definitely been a rewarding one. Through all the challenges, the pay off for Jeff has been being with his right partner, Theresa.

Jeff hopes that everyone who reads Men Are Like a Pair of Shoes will find the same happiness that he has been able to achieve in his own marriage. The author believes that anyone can find an ideal mate if they are willing to do the work of growing through what has been holding them back, revamping their dating approach and developing a well-thought-out, personalized Shopping List. This book is enriched by the insights Jeff has gained about people during his long sales career.

The author will be leading seminars and workshops based on the information in his book.

PART I

MEN = SHOES

There IS a Pair of Shoes For Everyone!

Are you wondering if you'll ever find your ideal mate? I believe there's someone for everyone. However, as a man observing the opposite sex, I've come to think that the reason many women are single or ill matched is that they haven't really figured out what they want. It's not, as the saying goes, that all the good guys are already hitched.

To know what you want, first you will need to understand yourself and think thoroughly about what would work for you in a romantic partner. Secondly, it's important not to get distracted by a man who isn't your right match. Lastly, you'll have to be persistent in your search for the right guy. You will be shown how to accomplish all this in *Men Are Like a Pair of Shoes.*

Why Shoes?

Some women I know were having problems with men and I was thinking one day about their relationships. I thought, if only these women would shop for a man the way they shop for a pair of shoes, their results would be better. I knew from my own experience that making adjustments in the way you search for a mate could make all the difference! I've been happily married for 13 years now, and it took two earlier marriages before I picked the right

woman—my current wife, Theresa. I found her only after I changed my approach to dating.

Because I've been there and now see so many people struggling with relationships, I decided to write this book. The reason I chose to write for single women, instead of men, is *women do the choosing.* Men ask, women have to accept for there to be a relationship.

The more I thought about the similarities between shopping for shoes and using a savvy approach to looking for the right man, the more I liked the comparison. In many ways, as you'll see in the pages ahead, the search for a man and a pair of shoes are very similar. Also, thinking about a man as a pair of shoes can take some of the sting out of your not having found the right guy yet.

Try it! Substitute the word "shoes" for "boyfriend" and see what this sounds like.

If this pair of shoes didn't hurt my feet so much, they would be perfect!

My shoes don't fit, but I'm still wearing them.

I can't live without this pair of shoes!

My shoes definitely need to change to the shoes I want.

I know they don't sell the shoes I want in this store, but I like shopping here.

I need new shoes, but I refuse to shop!

Do these comments sound as silly to you as they do to me as I write them? Yet, when you think of parallel statements that women make about their boyfriends, can't you think of someone who falls into each of these categories? Do you identify with one or more of them yourself?

What's the point of this exercise? By substituting the word "shoes" for "boyfriend," a woman can take a less emotional look at her romantic life, and as a result, see her situation more clearly. The truth is that it's more painful to put off a decision than to make it. Do you need to decide to make changes in your love life?

In *Men Are Like a Pair of Shoes: A Single Woman's Guide to Choosing Your Ideal Pair,* we're going to have some fun and consider some valuable lessons about relationships. We're going to compare your search for the right man to shopping for a great-fitting pair of supportive and durable shoes.

Now that you understand where we're coming from, I'll state my original belief in a new way: *There is a pair of shoes for every set of feet.* There are plenty of shoe stores in this world, right? And you'll find many types of shoes in those stores. Isn't that true? Well, the key to a successful shopping excursion is *knowing what you are looking for.* When you do, shopping will not only be fun, but also productive!

The goal of this book is to help you find the man you'll want to spend the rest of your life with. Is it time you changed your shopping habits? Have you been looking in the bargain basements when you really want to be shopping at the finest stores? If you're thinking of returning your current shoes, did you keep the receipt?

Shoe Fit Tip #1: Men are like a pair of shoes. While there are plenty of shoes to choose from in the stores, it takes some work to know what you need and to find the right pair. Think about your current shopping habits. Don't your feet deserve a pair of shoes that will be the right fit for the long term? That way, you won't have to march through life complaining, *oh, my aching feet!*

Select a Pair
That Will Fit You Tomorrow

Have you ever bought a pair of shoes that you loved? The shoes looked so great on your feet that you just had to wear them all the time. You wore those shoes everywhere, no matter where you were going or what you were doing. And you were pleased when you saw other people notice the shoes and how attractive they were.

However, with time, you realized that the shoes weren't really right for all the kinds of activities that you did, for all the places where you went, for all the new places you wanted to try.

Or perhaps your feet were starting to hurt because these shoes didn't provide enough arch support, crimped your toes, or rubbed and irritated your heel?

Soon you found that you were wearing the

shoes less and less—either because the novelty had worn off or because your feet were simply becoming too sore.

Or perhaps you didn't have time to shop for a while. As a result, you were stuck wearing those shoes for way too long.

Did you take more care in shopping the next time around? Or did you get caught up instead in the excitement of purchasing a new pair of shoes?

Shoes for a Lifetime

Now, let's raise the stakes. What if you knew that the next pair of shoes you were going to buy had to last for the rest of your life? How much time, effort and thought would you invest in shopping for those shoes?

Wouldn't you want to:

Learn what makes a quality shoe?

Educate yourself about the different shoe manufacturers?

Consider whether or not your feet needed to mend before you buy these shoes?

Make a list of your wants, needs and expectations?

Consider your options?

Discuss your possible choices with others?

Visit a ton of shoe stores beforehand?

As you can see buying the ideal shoes would take some time. You'd be learning both about yourself and about shoes. Along the way, you might make the wrong purchases out of impatience, pressure, or pure exhaustion. However, realizing that the shoes would have to last a lifetime, you'd quickly recognize your error and replace them. Overall, though, you'd be more thoughtful and thorough in your approach to shopping.

Shoe Fit Tip #2: When it comes to a lifetime pair of shoes (your mate), it's not enough that a pair is available for purchase; they've also got to fit your feet—today, tomorrow and in the years to come. *Men Are Like a Pair of Shoes* will help you make an informed choice. While it won't be supplying sources for FBI background checks (and hopefully you won't need them!), this book will assist you in:

Looking at your current shopping patterns

Moving on if your present shoes aren't the right fit

Getting back in the mood to shop if you've stopped

Considering the needs of your unique pair of feet

Preparing for wise shoe shopping

Thinking about the right stores to visit

Shopping smart based on your preparation

Caring for the shoes once you've found the right fit.

Now let's move on to Part II, "Women's Shoe Shopping & Ownership Habits." In Part II, we'll look at nonproductive patterns women fall into that prevent them from finding the right shoe fit.

PART II

WOMEN'S SHOE SHOPPING & OWNERSHIP HABITS

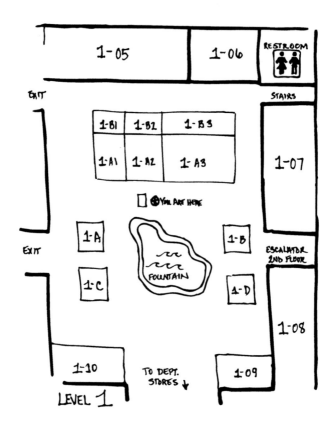

You Are Here!

Picture yourself at the mall. You're standing in front of one of those maps that tell you where you are currently located. Looking at that map and seeing the words "You are here" gives you a starting point. You know where you're starting from so you'll have a better chance of getting to where you want to go.

Think of this Part II as a mall map that's charting your romantic life. Each section in Part II is a different location on that map. Read through this part of the book to figure out where you are *right now*. (You may also recognize some places where you've been in an earlier period.)

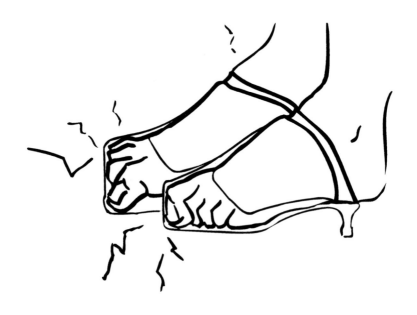

CURRENT
SHOE OWNERS

Are You Thinking about Throwing Out the Old Pair and Shopping for New Shoes?

Is something bothering you about your current pair of shoes? Have you been putting up with the discomfort of a wrong fit, discouraged by the effort involved in shopping for and adjusting to a new pair? Are you considering tossing them and shopping for new ones? For many shoe owners, it's indecision that keeps them hobbling unsteadily along, rather than striding forward comfortably in shoes that fit well.

There are many ways that you can get locked into a wrong, long-lasting shoe relationship:

*Telling yourself that these shoes are perfect, but...
(fill in the blank, if you dare face the truth!)*

*Trying to change the shoes you have into the
shoes you want*

*Wearing the wrong shoes because your mother,
friends,family, etc., tell you how right they are for
you (even when you know better)*

Continuing to wear shoes that are worn out

*Getting caught up in the excitement that an attractive
bold and daring pair of shoes brings into your
life.*

    If you're feeling stuck in any of these ways,
reading the related sections in Part II will help
you sort through whether a future shoe-shopping
trip is in your best interests. (Before shopping,
though, you and your current shoes would have
to face the fact that you won't be striding off into
the sunset together. Breaking up is the hard part,
and a lot less fun than the shopping phase.)
    Or maybe you're happy with shoes that will
only be in your life temporarily? Remember,
though, that it's easy to get attached to the "for
now only" shoes and end up trying to make them
into something they're not—namely, shoes that
will last a lifetime.
    Alternatively, it could be that your current
shoes are a fine fit; it's just that you haven't been
giving them the attention they deserve. Is your

shoe relationship just in need of repair? To consider this possibility, read the next section, "Is It
Time for a Shoe Repair Pit Stop?" Maybe there's
still a possibility that you can "keep on truckin'"
in the same shoes after a "polish or two."

Is It Time for a Shoe Repair Pit Stop?

Have you and your shoes been just limping along because of problems that have developed in the relationship? Have you lost that sense of excitement you used to have when you wore your shoes? Do you daydream about the good ol' days just after you first made this purchase? Do you find that you're even often walking around barefoot because the shoes have become increasingly uncomfortable?

If you're relating to this, it sounds like you and your shoes have reached a crossroads. Ask yourself whether you should keep hiking down the Road of Love together after a pit stop for repairs, or if it's time to part with the shoes and visit a rest stop alone. To help you sort it out, consider the following questions:

Is it simply an issue of giving your shoe relationship more attention?

Have you stopped doing the little things that make your shoes feel appreciated?

Would setting aside more time for your shoes help?

Could input from a shoe expert help renew the relationship and put that spring back in your step? Or...

Have you been avoiding dealing with the sore points because you sense the problems can't be fixed?

It's easy to take your shoes for granted once they become a regular part of your routine. Do your shoes feel unappreciated or vice versa? Is this shoe relationship worth the effort it would take to repair it? Do you want to continue this journey through life together?

When problems come up in a shoe relationship, it's actually an opportunity to bring what you have to a higher level. If you and the shoes can figure out how to handle your current sore points, it will form a basis for fixing future problems. You'll spend less time trudging down the Road of Love in pain and more time strolling along happily. However, this won't happen if you ignore the discomfort, simply hoping it will go away. Ignoring the pain is likely to simply result in sorer feet and less time spent in the shoes.

Men Are Like a Pair of Shoes is written primarily

for women who **want** to go shoe shopping. The sections in Part II explore the various patterns that keep us from having a successful shoe relationship. If you feel it's time to move on, keep reading Part II. If you want to stick with your current shoes and work it out, see the "Resources" and "Suggested Reading" sections in the back of this book for assistance.

Have You Been Thinking, These Shoes Are Perfect, But... ?

They're too tight! The heel's too tall! These "flimsy" shoes don't support my feet! I want a more practical color! My shoes have no flair! There's a multitude of reasons why you might be having second thoughts about your current pair of shoes.

Have you been downplaying these thoughts of doubt, that sensation that maybe the shoes you're wearing are not right for you? Are you insisting that the shoes are really perfect, and that the "buts" don't matter? Are you trying to convince yourself that:

It's not important if my shoes aren't ideal. They're there on my feet—aren't they?

I'd rather make do with this pair than have to walk around barefoot.

I'll never find another pair of shoes that I like this much.

Have you seen the shoes that they're trying to sell these days?

I'm going to have to settle for this current pair even though they don't really fit me because these may be the best shoes I will ever have.

Maybe you bought the shoes at a low point in your life. Did you shop in a hurry? Did you go with one of the first pairs that seemed to fit? Did you forget to consider what your real shoe needs would be over the long term? Were there early warning signs of a bad fit that you chose to ignore?

Are you now trying to convince yourself that you could live happily ever after with these shoes? Is Billy Joel's famous song, "I Love You Just the Way You Are," playing in your head? Could you be lying to yourself and ignoring the fact that your feet are painfully sore?

No one should have to be miserable and make do with a pair of shoes that aren't right for them. Are you trying to get your feet to fit the shoe in order to keep them on your feet? HELLO! They're just a pair of shoes. Shoes are manufactured to protect, pamper, and provide comfort to your feet. So, what's wrong with this picture?

Everyone deserves a pair of shoes that fit!

Shoe Fit Tip #3: Sometimes we refuse to acknowledge that a relationship isn't working until it completely breaks down or reality forces us to deal with the truth. Do you want to suddenly be left along the Freeway of Life with no shoes? Wouldn't it be easier to take a long hard look at your current pair of shoes and see them for what they are? To break up as your own choice in your own way? If you're in pain, the shoes are probably also unhappy being on your feet. You'd be doing both of you a favor.

Have You Been Trying to Change the Shoes You Have into the Shoes You Want?

Have you ever stood in front of a mirror and looked at shoes from different angles, telling yourself that this pair is not that bad. Maybe the things you don't like about them will change!

Do you think that if you take excellent care of the shoes, they will **want** to change for you? You could be so incredibly good to them that they'll have no choice but to change? Their needs could never be met the way that they are with you.

When this approach doesn't work, you might start to ask the shoes to change. You might feel bad about this because you believe they should know what your needs are. The shoes make a half-hearted attempt to change, or only pay lip service to doing the things you ask. You want to believe the shoes can change, but deep down some doubts start to develop.

Since asking directly hasn't produced much progress, you may begin to covertly manipulate the shoes into changing. Instead of improving the fit, the shoes now become even more uncomfortable "under this new weight." You'd understandably grow increasingly frustrated. Don't the shoes understand how perfect life would be if only they would make the changes you're asking for?

Finally, as a last measure you threaten to discard the shoes. Maybe threats are the only way to force them to do what you want. However, these threats don't bring the change you want. So one day you load the shoes into your car to take them to the local thrift store. On the drive there, you covertly eye the shoes looking for any last minute hope for change, but they, nonchalantly, stay **exactly the same**. Then, at the store, you study the shoes intently in front of a mirror one last time to see if your threat has had any effect. Nope now there's no hope in your heart because the shoes still won't change!

A few days later, however, you sheepishly find yourself back in the thrift store checking on whether or not the shoes have sold. Are they willing to change now? **No!** Well, even though the shoes are still the same bad fit, you wonder if you should hurry up and buy them again before they end up on someone else's feet. Maybe you just haven't tried the right approach to making the shoes change...

Shoe Fit Tip #4: No matter where you are in this painful process of trying to change your current pair of uncomfortable shoes, it's a no win situation. While you and your "footwear" may develop skills that can improve your relationship, his "sole" is not going to change. Is your issue something achievable—like quitting smoking—or is this problem area an integral part of who the shoe is? What is your man's style? Does his style match **your** personality and needs? If not, maybe it's time to move on so you can develop the skills to find a better-suited pair. That way, you may well discover what's holding you back from finding a pair of shoes that will be right for you over the long term.

Are You Wearing Shoes
Someone Else Chose for You?

Did you go shopping for shoes with a friend or relative and end up buying the pair that *they* thought was right for you? In the pressure of the moment, you valued their judgment more than your own and, as a result, took home the pair of shoes they said suited you best? Or maybe you were lazy and even allowed them to go do the shopping without you?

However, it wasn't the friend or relative who had to wear those shoes every day, was it? It was you. And what happened? With time, did you get in touch with what you needed and saw that those shoes just weren't it?

Now you're wearing ill-fitting shoes that are making you miserable. That means you'll have to part with the shoes and go through the whole shoe selection process all over again. Plus you'll need time to get over your "love hangover" before you shop. Wouldn't it have made more sense to know what you want so you could have picked the right shoes yourself the first time around?

Sometimes friends or relatives give us their opinions with good intentions. In other cases, people are selfish and tend to give advice that is more self-serving than beneficial to us. In either situation, it's important to give more weight to our own good judgment than what others tell us to do. For who knows better what's right for us than ourselves?

For example, would you allow someone else to:

Select all of your clothes?

Pick your hairstyle?

Decide if you should take a new job?

Of course not! While you might consider the suggestions of others, you'd make the final decision. So why would you allow them to select one of your most important items—your shoes?

Asking friends and relatives their opinion is different than allowing them to make up your mind for you. Of course we want to select shoes that will fit in with the community of people who are in our lives. It's very difficult to wear shoes that are always causing trouble for us with other people. On the other hand, it's great when parents, other relatives and friends like our shoes and get along well with them.

Note: It's true that another person might suggest a shoe match that is a good choice for you. However, it's essential that the final decision be yours and that it resonate with all that you know about yourself and your needs.

Men Are Like a Pair of Shoes will help you figure out what qualities your ideal shoes should have. If you've been having trouble making wise shoe choices for yourself in the past, you'll be better equipped than ever to do so by the time you finish reading this book!

Shoe Fit Tip #5: Today there are popular TV shows for which the producers select possible dating or mating candidates for show participants. On these dating shows, the result often is more hilarious than successful. So even when TV producers screen thousands of applicants, they have trouble finding that one person an individual could stay with for the rest of their life.

What does this tell us? It's saying that *we need to make our own informed decisions.* How can anyone else choose the partner who will be right for you for life? No matter how well our friends or relatives know us, there's no one in a better position to know what you need than yourself. The final decision **must** be yours.

Are You Wearing Another Woman's Shoes?

Jane thought she had found the perfect pair of shoes. They just appeared magically one day in her life. Looking around, she didn't see an owner so she tried them on. To her surprise, they fit well. These shoes were very comfortable and she could walk in them for hours. It was just so much fun for her to wear these shoes, and she could tell that the shoes were also having a great time being on her feet. Plus the shoes would surprise Jane with flowers and other gifts and they didn't mind splurging on expensive meals.

Jane was a bit confused when the shoes would disappear for a while, but they always showed up again before too long. Since she felt so special when she wore these shoes, she overlooked

these disappearances and ignored that little warning voice inside. Jane had never felt better wearing
any other pair of shoes she ever had and she told
herself that maybe the shoes just needed encour-
agement because they had been hurt in the past.

But that little warning voice persisted as Jane
noticed a few other odd things. It seemed that the shoes
were only willing to go certain places and could see Jane
only at very specific times. In addition, the one phone
number the shoes would give Jane is for their cellular
phone. *Really, this is the best number to use to reach me,* the
shoes said. Hmmmm... Adding up all the signs, Jane
was finally forced to "see the light" and realized that
these shoes might belong to someone else.

Jane confronted the shoes, and they boldly
admitted that she was right. Another woman
owns them! However the shoes said that this was
no reason for her not to wear them. *Don't I fit you
well and aren't you having a great time?* The shoes
also told Jane that maybe if all goes well, they'll
decide that they want to be owned *by her alone.*
They'll end the other shoe relationship in time if it
feels right and commit to only being on her feet.
This sounded somewhat reasonable to Jane in the
haze of shoe lust.

Jane felt lonely and unappreciated during
those periods when she and the shoes were apart,
but the fun and excitement of their times together
seemed to make up for it. Meanwhile she found
herself feeling jealous of a girlfriend who has
shoes that are committed only to her. And, even
worse, one night Jane saw "her" shoes out on
their real owner's feet! At first she was shocked,

but over time Jane convinced herself that the shoes didn't look like they were having a very good time.

Caught up in her feelings for these shoes, she kept wearing them when she could. Jane even justified it by telling herself how convenient this shoe relationship is. *Don't I have the best of both worlds? I get to see the shoes, but don't have the major responsibility for them yet. I'm really not ready and don't have the time now anyway. And when it's right, the shoes are going to commit to me, aren't they?*

Eventually Jane spends the time apart scheming up ways to make the shoes feel so special that they'll decide to choose her exclusively. She does this even though, in the back of her mind, she worries the shoes might eventually stray to another pair of feet once they're on hers. Jane tells herself this couldn't possibly happen because she and the shoes are so right for each other.

Shoe Fit Tip #6: Few relationships are as primed to trigger longing and obsession in a woman as the affair with the married, or otherwise unavailable, man. All that time by yourself fuels the fantasy that he is the *only one* for you. And for a woman who hasn't worked through her own fears of commitment, the married man presents the perfect partner to blame for not being fully attached. Might your choice partly be the result of needing to feel better about yourself? Wake up! It's time to see that you deserve a man of your own.

As long as you're putting up with the

arrangement and not causing problems, you may be the only likely person to end this affair. Get unstuck and let go. If the support of your friends isn't enough, see a therapist to help you through the letting go process. The real shoe relationship you want isn't a part-time, shared deal because that just stinks.

"I Have to Have Them!
I Have to Have Them!"

Strolling down the street one sunny day on your lunch hour, you spotted a shoe store. Glancing in the window, you noticed the most handsome pair of shoes that you had ever seen. In fact, these shoes were so gorgeous that you stopped dead in your tracks. It felt like butterflies were in your stomach. *It must be fate,* you told yourself. *I've got to have these shoes!* Then you rushed inside to try on the shoes quickly before you needed to be back at work.

When you told the clerk which shoes you wanted, she smiled. The clerk asked if you wanted to try on any others, and you said, "No, these are the ones I want." Anxiously you waited to see if the store had your size. While waiting, you noticed the exorbitant price on the floor model and decided you didn't care. ***I have to have them!*** you thought. *I have to have them!* What a relief it was when you saw your shoe size on the outside of the box that the clerk was carrying!

After the clerk brought the pair over to you, you observed that the shoes were even more handsome up close! You admired them in the box for a moment, and then nervously tried both shoes on. Wow, you couldn't believe how great they looked on your feet! It kind of took your breath away. You sat still a moment to regain your composure, and then tried walking around. While the shoes rubbed your heel a little, you hardly noticed because they were so good-looking.

The first day out in those shoes was so exhilarating! You felt like a new person, so happy and bright. You couldn't stop smiling. And you keep looking down at your feet to make sure the shoes were really there! You couldn't believe your luck. The shoes were so stunning! While they were irritating your heel a little, you thought that would go away once they were broken in.

Eventually you introduced the shoes to your best friend at a party. The whole night you noticed that she couldn't seem to take her eyes off the shoes. Your friend wasn't the only one looking. All the women at the party noticed these shoes. After that party, your best friend kept telling you how lucky you were to be with shoes that are that handsome! She asked how they fit, and you told her that your heel was a bit sore. Your friend gave you a lot of advice about dealing with that sort of problem.

Finally you took the shoes home to meet your parents. Everyone seemed to get along and have a good time. The next day, though, your parents called to bring up some concerns they had about the shoes. You admitted that your heel was sore but insisted this wasn't a big issue. (You didn't mention the bill that you were still paying off!) Your parents suggested that you think about this relationship and whether it's the right one for you.

Except for your parents, everyone else has the same response to the shoes. "Your shoes are so handsome," they all say. You love hearing it and still agree. Wouldn't it be great to wake up every day for the rest of your life to find these handsome shoes waiting for you? Now if you could only do something to stop them from irritating your heel...

Shoe Fit Tip #7: Focusing on physical attraction as the lone criteria for being with a partner is dangerous. Intoxicated by the physical chemistry, you might be blinded to potential problems that could cause you plenty of heartache in the long run. While chemistry is important, there are a lot of other factors that you need to also look for in a mate—consideration, loyalty, sense of humor, attitude, stability, etc. We'll be exploring these qualities and others in later sections of *Men Are Like a Pair of Shoes.*

Are you putting too much emphasis on your shoe's physical appearance? Are you interpreting attraction as love? Are you really seeing this relationship for what it is? Begin to take a good look at *who* this man is, not just what he looks like. Does he have many good qualities to bring to your relationship, or have you just been high on the attraction between the two of you? If the latter is true, move on and learn to balance chemistry with quality in your future romantic relationships.

Are You Keeping Your Shoes a Secret?

Maybe you didn't notice it right away. You just met the shoes, and the two of you started spending time together. At first, it seemed inconvenient to introduce them to your friends, and you always wait a while before mentioning new shoes to your mother or other family members.

But then, as time went on, you never seemed to get around to mentioning your shoes to anyone. One day it dawned on you. *You are embarrassed that you have wearing these shoes!* You really don't want to admit it to anyone. Yet there's something that keeps you hanging on to this shoe relationship.

My advice? If the shoes are good enough to have in your life, they should be good enough to talk about and eventually introduce to friends and family. What have you been thinking?

There are many reasons that we end up in shoe relationships that we're too embarrassed to tell the world about. These include:

👠 *The desire for a rebound relationship to serve as glue for a shattered ego*

👠 *Life pressures that are unusually hard to deal with*

👠 *Low self-esteem*

👠 *Financial problems*

👠 *Loneliness*

When you're there, but not really there, in a shoe relationship, you're cheating both of you of the possibility of a better match. On some level, the shoes probably have sensed how poorly you think of them. You're not really playing fair. This is basically "using" someone for your own needs and not thinking about their feelings.

Instead of soothing yourself with "only good for the moment" shoes, you've got to face whatever issue is pushing you into their arms. Maybe this isn't something you can deal with on your own, and it requires a therapist's help. Or perhaps you just need to find more "feet friends" to offer you emotional support.

Rather than feeling bad about the shoes, and therefore probably also about yourself, you could be improving your life and bringing it to a higher level. That way, you'll be able to attract shoes into your life that you'll want brag about.

Let the shoes go. There are many more shoes in the mall. You don't have to settle for the bargain store special.

Shoe Fit Tip #8: By involving the shoes in your life, you have probably given them the impression that you consider this to be a real relationship with some potential. Be kind and stop fueling false hope on the *shoes'* part. Besides, could being with these shoes really be so great if you feel you have to hide them from the world?

STILL SHOPPING?

Can't Get Real Satisfaction from Your Current Shopping Style?

Is that classic Rolling Stones tune—"I Can't Get No Satisfaction"— your theme song? Are you single and shopping, but have a funny feeling that you need to change your approach? You've been actively "in the mall" time and time again, but you're never satisfied with your purchases. Sure, shopping is fun, but this has its limits. After a while, you want to have a consistent pair of shoes around.

This section "Still Shopping" looks at nonproductive patterns shoppers get into when they're still in the "looking around" phase. Perhaps you're not committed to a particular pair of shoes right now and you'll recognize yourself in one of the three examples that are presented. Do you find that...

You're always attracted to the same shoe type over and over again, even when you try to change it?

You play at shopping and avoid getting too deeply involved with any one pair of shoes?

You're in a phase in which you're buying (sleeping with) lots of shoes, but seem to often end up wanting more commitment than you're getting from this type of shoe relationship?

You can't work on changing your behavior if you are not aware of what you do. When you're not satisfied with the results you're getting from your shopping trips it makes sense to take a closer look at how you're behaving. Once you've identified your pattern, you can use your current frustration as fuel for creating change.

Yes, you'll need to be willing to change on a deep level before you will truly commit to behaving differently. Think about whether there could be some sort of payoff from how you're acting right now. Can you see that whatever it is, the price has become too high, as evidenced in your increasing frustration? Can you imagine a time when your shopping habits could bring deeper and more satisfying rewards? Could it be time to let go of your nonproductive pattern and whatever payoffs you've felt it has provided?

Don't worry! Help is at hand. Just turn the page....

Have You Been Shopping at the Wrong Store?

Have you been doing your shoe shopping at the wrong kind of store? Once you're there, do you pick the same type of shoe over, and over, and over again? Do the shoes end up treating your feet in the same negative way—eventually?

Or maybe you tried to shop at a different kind of store to purchase a new style of shoes. However, when you got home, you got a sinking feeling in your stomach as you realized that the new pair was basically identical to the ones you've been buying at the old place?

In many ways, you feel like you've been wearing the same type of bad-fit shoes for most of your life. When you boil it down, all those shoes could have just been one, uncomfortable pair— they were that much alike!

If your tired from the pain you might be asking yourself: *Why am I always wearing the same type of shoes? I know that this kind of shoe doesn't work for me, but I buy similar ones again and again.*

Obviously there's something attracting you to this shoe type. Whatever the criteria is, it isn't a sound one for you. Are you picking fun, open sandals even though you live in a cold, snowy climate? Do you favor active, daredevil shoes, despite the fact that they take you on risky adventures? What is your shoe type? Can you see what faulty reasoning you might currently be basing your choices on?

Buying similar shoes at the same store is OK when the shoes you purchase treat your feet well. If your current sort of shoe relationship is productive and comfortable for you, fine—in fact, that's great! The problem is when you're always attracted to a certain type of shoe and, as a result, continually have a bad outcome.

If you're a woman who feels she's been drawn to the wrong type of shoe in the past, I've got good news for you. The fact that you're questioning your choices now is a major breakthrough! Seeing that your shopping approach and shoe type need to change is a revelation that can have a huge, positive impact on your life.

Shopping at different stores *with better criteria* will improve your results. Part of creating a change in your life will also involve looking at what care *your feet* need before you go to the mall to shop.

Shoe Fit Tip #9: The easiest way to try to change your current pattern is to go right out to a new store with the intention of buying something different. However, to make a real change, you'll need to look at your current shopping criteria and determine if some previous wounds might influence it. If so, even if you shopped in a new type of atmosphere, you'd be likely to go for shoes with the same old style! Many times, there's healing that needs to take place before we can make healthier choices. Consider whether this is true for you. (You'll find more on healing in later sections.) In addition, by reading *Men Are Like a Pair of Shoes,* you will develop the skills of both picking the right stores and the right shoes.

Are You Just "Window Shopping"?

Have you just been passing time in the mall, looking at the footwear displayed in the windows of shoe stores? Are you simply trying shoes on, or do you actually want to purchase a new pair? There's a difference between *just shopping* and *shopping to buy*. Let's think of *"window shoppers"* as those women who are stuck somewhere in the shopping cycle because they're not really serious about buying shoes.

To see if this describes you, it will be helpful to review the shopping process. A shoe shopper needs to look at possible selections before she can make a purchase, right? And as the shopper is looking, she'll probably try on some of the shoes. Unless the shoes are placed on her feet, how will she know which pair makes the best fit? Many wise shoe shoppers also meander around the aisles in the candidate shoes to see if they feel comfortable during a short, initial trial-run.

It's obvious that looking at footwear is an essential phase in the shoe shopping process. But are you stuck at this shopping stage or at another step in the shopping cycle? "Just shopping" is a good excuse for not choosing one particular pair. You tell yourself that:

I'm just looking right now to get a better idea of what I want.

I've been shopping, but haven't seen anything I like enough to buy yet.

I'm having fun just shopping; I really don't think I need a permanent pair of shoes to make me complete anymore.

The trial runs are enough for me at the moment; later I'll make a shoe commitment.

There's really nothing worth buying, but I keep hoping my shoes are out there somewhere!

As author Gail Sheehy wrote, everyone goes through different "passages" in their lives. There are times when it's perfectly natural to just want to "window shop." But be honest with yourself. Is there something stopping you from taking your shoe relationships to the next level? Are you really satisfied by just shopping? Or have you been kidding yourself that this is the right stage for you?

While shopping is an important part of finding the right shoes, it's meant to be a means to an end. If you really want something more, what's holding you back?

Shoe Fit Tip #10: Have you sensed that you're not satisfied with "just shopping," or is this possibility a new idea for you? While men are generally considered the ones to be wary of commitment, there are plenty of commitment-phobic women out there too. Women also face conflicts between their desire to connect (buy one pair of shoes) and their fears of how much they will need to compromise (the price) to have the relationship.

Shopping can be a great way to enjoy some companionship and have fun while you're single. But if your goal is to find your ideal shoes and you're stuck in the shopping phase, maybe it's time to work through the fears that a shoe commitment stirs in you. While shopping is fun, there are rewards that will come from making a buying decision. (In particular, see the sections, "Heal Thy Feet" and "Paying for Your Shoes.")

Have You Been Buying Too Many Pairs?

It takes all kinds of feet to make a world, and when you're a single woman who's shopping, decisions about how quickly to "buy" (**in this section, I'm using "buy" to refer to "sleeping with"**) a pair of shoes and how many pairs to buy are really individual ones. Your choices will be influenced by your age, religious beliefs, cultural influences, current circumstances, etc.

However, in this age of instant gratification, some shoppers need a reminder that casual shoe buying can end up costing more than just the number stated on the price tag. Some people would say: *"If it feels good, do it."* However, I think it's better to ask yourself the question: *"While this may feel great now, will I feel good about it tomorrow?"*

How a woman will feel about casual buying emotionally is a multi-pronged issue. First, there are your own feelings to consider. If the purchase creates just one night of pleasure or an ongoing, casual physical connection, will you end up expecting more than this type of relationship often delivers? If you get less than you expect or hope for, it's likely that you'll end up feeling hurt and somewhat used.

The second side of the emotional issue is the shoe's reaction to the purchase. While some casual purchases lead to a deeper, lasting relationship, this buy comes with no guarantees, and the odds are against it.

The major problem with casual buying is that it often occurs before the shoes and the shopper really have a good sense of what each party is bringing to the connection. The purchase rushes a level of intimacy that neither party is really ready for. This is often what makes both of you feel uncomfortable in these situations and why you end up parting.

In addition, there's the problem of foot diseases (STDs, really). If the shoe encourages a quick purchase, who knows how many other deals like this there have been and whether they were safe ones? The diseases you can get range from mildly annoying infections, to warts and herpes, which reoccur, to the deadly AIDS. So if you do decide to make a playful purchase just for the fun, do play safe (see "Suggested Reading" for info).

The bottom line? *What are you really after?* Making quick purchases and expecting the shoes to end up saying, "I do" is not a wise approach. If an ideal pair of lifetime-lasting shoes is what you're wanting, it will be smarter to take the time to really know the shoes before getting that close. And, if you find you want to make that purchase, focus on that one shoe relationship to see where it may go.

Shoe Fit Tip #11: The worst matches between women and their shoes occur when the expectations of each party are widely different. If you're looking for your ideal pair of shoes, picking ones that push for a quick sale is likely to lead to disappointment. And if you don't play it safe, this behavior can also lead to disease.

Have you made some quick purchases lately and regretted it? Maybe look at what's driving your behavior. Are you lonely? Are you hoping to secure the relationship by offering sex? Do you need to look at these situations more realistically? Is it time for you to learn to be close to your shoes in other ways? While sex is important, there are many aspects to a relationship beyond the bedroom.

SINGLE,
BUT *NOT* SHOPPING

Have You Been Walking Around Barefoot?

First, I want to point out that there's nothing inherently wrong with walking around barefoot. It feels good to brush against the green grass in your bare feet, or to hike down the beach without shoes or socks, splashing in the incoming waves. There are times when it makes perfectly good sense just to have fun as an unattached pair of feet and not to take on the responsibility of a shoe relationship. Some people are content to go shoeless for most of their lives. This is a decision that we all need to make for ourselves.

Assuming that most shoppers, though, want to buy footwear, I'd also like to suggest that bare-foot readers look at their reasons for not wearing shoes. Do you find yours in the following list?

Do you feel that you're not ready for a shoe commitment?

Do you have unique demands in your life right now that need your full attention?

Have you not found shoes yet that are worthy of you?

Has a shoe relationship ended recently, so you're taking time off from shopping?

Being barefoot a while for any of these reasons usually makes a lot of sense. However, if you've been avoiding buying shoes for quite some time now because of fears, hang-ups or old wounds, it's probably time to deal with them. Or if you're discouraged or put off by the process of shopping, maybe you need a new approach. You don't have to stay stuck in a holding pattern.

For more on these "holding pattern" situations, see the later sections in Part II titled:

Have You Given Up on Shopping?

Have You Been Afraid to Shop?

Have Your Feet Been Mending?

Do You Hate to Shop?

Since you're in the barefoot stage right now, you might as well as take advantage of having more time for you. Seize the moment and use your freedom to explore life! This is a great time to get to know yourself better and to discover the things you enjoy doing the most.

If you do the barefoot trip right, your feet will feel relaxed and secure, ready to go shoe shopping. Don't forget to use some of this time to refine your Shopping List!

Have You Given Up On Shopping?

Maybe you've been barefoot a little too long. The initial excitement of it has certainly worn off. Lately, weekends have been filled up with errands, a girls night out, and rented videos. Shopping may seem like a distant, fading memory from a former life. Once in a while, you may feel a pang of hurt because it's been soooooooo long since you've had your own pair of shoes. Even so, the effort of shopping just seems like *too much work!* Have you given up?

While you keep telling yourself to make the effort to shop, instead you've been avoiding the mall. Do you really know why you're not shopping?

Was your approach not leading you to any shoes that you liked?

Have you felt overwhelmed by work, school or family obligations?

Are your girlfriends all in relationships, so there's no one to shop with?

Are you at a loss about which stores have the right shoes for you?

Sometimes moving ahead in life just requires some education. All of the reasons above could be canceled out with a little research. For instance...

Absorbing the content in "Men Are Like a Pair of Shoes" can help you devise an approach to shopping that will lead you to the right places that will have quality footwear.

Reading books on creating balance in life and setting limits with others (see "Suggested Reading") can assist you in finding some free time for shopping.

Becoming a member of a local women's support group, attending some fun classes related to your hobbies, and joining organizations that offer meetings and activities can result in making new single women friends who like to shop and share your other interests. (You might also spot a nice pair of shoes along the way!)

While all of this takes some time, with patience you can make progress.

No one likes to feel like they've failed. Yet sometimes failing is exactly what we need to do in order to discover that it's time to change our ways. If you're feeling discouraged, be easy on yourself. Find even some small ways to begin to move forward. Start journaling to explore issues that may be roadblocks to your progress. Learn to meditate in order to reduce your stress and to gain insight into your behavior.

In Part III, you'll find more advice on the process of preparing to shop.

Shoe Fit Tip #12: While being discouraged about the potential success of your future shopping efforts is understandable, you'll need to learn to motivate yourself in order to get back to the mall with the right attitude. One helpful way is to start thinking about what it could be like to spend time with the right shoes, instead of just sitting around feeling bad about your prospects. Creating the Shopping List in Part III will bring a positive image of the future into sharper focus.

Have You Been Afraid to Shop?

Have your past experiences with shoes made you fearful about shopping again? Certainly wearing ill-fitting shoes can be painful and you might feel protective of your feet. You may also find that you're blaming all those shoes for your bad experiences. You start expecting relationships with new shoes to be just the same old sad story.

If you are relating to this, I suggest that you ask yourself an important question. It will

help you see that you've had a part in creating
the pain. That *you chose* to wear the shoes! Isn't it
true that you could have stopped wearing any of
the shoes in your past? In most cases I think your
answer will be "Yes."

Once that question and answer has sunk
in, you'll begin to see that you have a responsibility for the quality of your shoe relationships. Did
the way you shopped in the past usually result in
having bad-fitting shoes? Doesn't it make sense to
come up with a better approach to shopping?
That way, you won't have to feel stuck with a
negative outcome.

Certainly you're not the only shopper who
has ever kept wearing uncomfortable shoes. Most
of us have done this at some point. In fact, you
probably have a friend right now who's wearing
bad-fit shoes that she tried to discard earlier.
Maybe you have another friend who quit wearing
one pair of ill suited shoes only to find another
set just like them. It's as if your friends are walking on a treadmill going nowhere. These friends
are stepping along, so they *think* that they're getting somewhere. Yet the treadmill is stationary—
your friends are actually stuck in one place!

What about *your* last pair of shoes? Were
they a couch potato that always changed your
plans to go out at the last minute so you two
could just hang out at home? Did they upset you
during periods when you had important responsibilities at work, with your family, or elsewhere?
Were they just not there at crucial times when
you needed their support? Blaming your shoes for

their contributions to making a relationship dis-
appointing is OK, at first. However, it's essential
that you soon move on to taking responsibility
for creating a better relationship with a new kind
of shoe.

Once you realize that you can avoid such
unnecessary pain before it starts, a welcomed
sense of relief will come over you. You are taking
responsibility for your life! That's great! Now part
of that responsibility will be learning how to find
and buy a different type of shoe. You'll be looking
for shoes that will pamper and appreciate your
feet—not take them for granted or abuse them.

Shoe Fit Tip #13: Blaming shoes for your past
pain can make you feel better for a while.
However it's not a productive pastime over the
long run. Once you see that certain shoes are
going to be uncomfortable, take responsibility for
learning how to find a different type of shoe. This
step is crucial to your moving forward into a
more positive future. Take some time to reflect on
why the shoes in your past were wrong for you.
What qualities would a better pair have? You'll
find help for creating a new Shopping List in Part
III.

Have Your Feet
Been Mending?

Did your last pair of shoes hurt your feet
and you don't feel ready yet to try on any new
ones? Certainly healing your feet after parting
with a pair of shoes is necessary. Your feet need
time to heal.

Deciding to take a break after ending a
shoe relationship can be a positive decision. We
usually need some time to step back and figure
out why you and the shoes weren't a good match.
Time off gives us a chance to reflect on the dis-
carded shoe relationship as we heal. Plus shopping for new shoes could be emotionally drain-
ing, and for a while, you need that energy for
yourself.

Some shoppers don't realize that they need
a break between shoes, and they go out to the
mall too soon. While trying on the new shoes,
their feet hurt, signaling the shopper that they're
not ready. Even so, they forge on ahead, only to
have the unacknowledged pain disrupt the poten-

tiality of a new shoe relationship.

How can you bolster the mending process? For some shoppers, a support group will be a good place to vent the feelings of disappointment, anger and sadness that come up after a parting. When we hear the other support group members' stories, we feel less alone. You'll see that they're going through the same transition. Coping strategies are shared too. You may also make some new friends or more...

Actually, I took a lot of time off after my first two marriages failed, and eventually attended a support group for divorced Catholics. That's where my lovely wife Theresa and I met and made the initial connection that eventually led to our harmonious marriage.

While you may not find your new shoes in a support group, it can be part of your strategy to keep your feet busy. And, in addition to the support group, consider fun new activities too—including those connected to hobbies you've always wanted to pursue. The social activities will help keep your mood upbeat, and they can prevent you from calling the old shoes and maybe getting back into a relationship you know wouldn't work.

Eventually your reflective time must focus on the ways you contributed to the downside of your shoe relationship and how you can make a better selection in shoes the next time around. This is part of taking responsibility for the quality of your shoe relationships (a subject that was discussed in "Have You Been Afraid to Shop?"). Note that taking responsibility is different than being hard on yourself. Being hard on yourself sounds like this: *"I should have loved the shoes more, then everything would have been alright."* Taking responsibility sounds like: *"I bought the shoes. I did not have to buy those particular shoes."*

Even before a shoe purchase, a shopper might have a feeling that buying a particular pair of shoes could lead to problems. For whatever reason, the shopper overlooks it. Later she sees that it was a mistake not to listen to her gut feelings. This may or may not have been the case for you. Either way, you now have an opportunity to channel your hard-earned wisdom into positive action. *Reading Men Are Like a Pair of Shoes* is part of your bright new direction. You *can and will* make better choices.

Shoe Fit Tip #14: While reflection is an important part of healing when you've parted with a pair of shoes, don't prolong the agony by pining over your great times together. Use the reflective time wisely to consider what went wrong, and as soon as possible, move on to what you could do better and how to make a smarter shoe selection next time. Also, do more than just sit around reflecting during the healing phase. Have some fun too. Reconnect with friends you lost touch with when you were with the shoes, join social groups and make new friends, and try out a new hobby or two. It will all add up to a more contented, less mournful you.

Do You Hate to Shop?

    Some feet just hate to shop. When it comes to getting a new pair of shoes, they dread going into the store and getting involved in the whole process of shopping. *Maybe I'll just magically bump into my pair of Mr. Right shoes one day in a crowded elevator,* the hate-to-shopper dreams. Or, *I know... I'll spot my ideal shoes at that museum lecture next week on European Impressionism, and it will be love at first sight!*

While anything could happen (and for some lucky feet, this type of scenario will occur), don't count on the ideal shoes just showing up one day. There's bound to be some shopping—some involvement in the process of elimination—before you'll be able to pick the shoes that are right for you. Let's say that those Mr. Right shoes did show up tomorrow. If you haven't put any thought into which shoes are ideal for you, you might not recognize the right shoes even if they were standing right in front of you! You might just walk on by in pursuit of shoes that are the same old style that always gets you into trouble!

Face it. For most of us, shopping is going to be part of the buying process—like it or not. So why not come up with a shopping approach that you think you would enjoy? If you do a good job of refining that dusty, old shopping approach you abandoned some time ago, you should end up having a great time. The reason? You'll be trying on shoes that have real potential of being the comfortable fit that you've dreamt about.

Maybe it's the images you have in your mind right now that make you hate to shop. Who would look forward to the discomfort of being tongue-tied over dinner with a pair of shoes you have nothing in common with. Or opening the front door only to eye a pair of shoes that remind you remarkably of your disastrous Ex? Or seeing on your doorstep any variation of the type of shoes you'd be miserable with?

Well, the good news is that the book you have in your hands is the perfect one for you.

Why *Men Are Like a Pair of Shoes?* Well, one of the main reasons I wrote this book was to help women think through their criteria for their ideal shoes so they could start making smarter purchases. That's why the Shopping List is a featured part of this book. It's my hope that women will find it useful in figuring out the type of shoe relationship that would last in their lives.

Shoe Fit Tip #15: If your ideal shoes are just around the corner (or just pages ahead of you), don't you think it's in your best interest to drop your "hate to shop" attitude? Maybe part of improving your perspective is brushing up on some skills that will make shopping less stressful for you. Work on some comfortable opening lines (starting with the easy winner, "Hello!"). Think about what you'd want to tell your ideal shoes about your life. What would you want to know about him? Where would you like to go? What would you like to do? What would you want to wear? How casual or formal would the whole shopping process feel? Come on, now. Isn't shopping already beginning to feel like a lot more fun? What if you *could buy* the shoes you want? Now you know what you've been doing wrong, how do you move in a more positive direction?

PART III

PREPARING TO SHOP SMART

Being the Right Pair of Feet

Before you can choose your ideal pair of shoes, you need to make sure you've become the right pair of feet.

Being the right pair of feet isn't just about getting pedicures and painting your toenails. Yes, looking attractive is important, but having the right feet requires more than that. You also need to do the personal work it will take to feel great about yourself and confident about the whole shopping process.

In Part II, we began to look at some of the issues women have about shopping. In Part III, we'll take some more time to cover the care your feet might need before you go looking for your ideal shoes. At the end of Part III, after addressing foot care, we'll move on to creating your Shopping List for your ideal match in shoes.

Why is having the right pair of feet so important? One important reason is that when it comes to shopping, strong confident feet attract strong, confident shoes. Healthy shoes will appreciate the foot care you've done. In contrast, feet in fine condition challenge unhealthy shoes, and they're likely to find a way to put the feet down for it!

In addition, wearing confident shoes usually will not make nervous feet feel confident. Apprehensive feet most often have difficulty wearing confident shoes and soon become tired of the effort of keeping up with them. The anxious feet begin to feel worse about themselves, and may begin to criticize the great shoes.

So take some time now to consider the condition of your feet. Are your feet all they could be? Are there areas of your life that need work? Could the poor condition of your feet be part of the reason you've attracted the wrong shoes in the past?

The shoes that will be drawn to you will reflect the state of your feet. Are you feeling proud and confident that you're ready for the shoes you've been dreaming of? If not, the following sections will help you get your feet ready for the ideal shoes. If you've already spent time working on yourself, you can soon move ahead to "What Type of Shoes Are You Really Looking For?" But first, read "Paying for Your Shoes" and if you have children, also see "Shoes for a Mother's Feet: Special Considerations."

Heal Thy Feet

Years of purchasing the wrong shoes signal a need for some tender, loving self-care for your feet. This is more than just caring for your feet after a specific breakup, as discussed in "Have Your Feet Been Mending?" Here we're talking about the healing that you may have needed in your life for some time and that you're now seeking in order to become the right feet for your ideal shoes.

Let's work on identifying the type of healing your feet might require.

Do you need to simply have better criteria for your shoe choices and that's why you're reading this book?

Is it time to get a clearer understanding of yourself so you can truly know what type of shoes you need?

Did you fall into one of the negative patterns identified earlier in the book for feet that are currently matched up with the wrong shoes?

Did you relate to one of the nonproductive dating patterns described in the "Still Shopping" section?

Has reading "Single But Not Shopping" clarified the issues that are keeping you out of the mall?

Could deeper issues be playing into your wrong choices?
Fear of commitment
Replaying of childhood trauma in order to "fix it"
Codependent behavior where you take care of the shoes while sacrificing your feet
(fill in the blank)

Is there a specific problem area of your life that is affecting your relationships?
Career transitions
Weak communication skills
Stress from being over-committed to work or family
(fill in the blank)

What's important is that you recognize your current pattern or problem and work on healing it. Heal thy feet, and then when you're feeling good about yourself, work on being able to make a better shoe choice the next time around.

A common mistake is to jump right out there and try to find a pair of shoes that do not hurt your feet the way your past shoes have. However, if you don't give your feet some care first, one of two things can happen. The new shoes may hurt your feet in a new way, doubling your pain. Or the bad condition of your feet can ruin a relationship with a great pair of shoes.

Healing your feet doesn't have to take years. Once you identify the specific issue that requires healing, get the help that you need to take care of it. You'll get a jump-start from both the "Resources" and "Suggested Reading" sections in the back of this book.

Shoe Fit Tip #16: While time can heal your wounds, you need to identify what these are for you. What issues have held you back from a lasting, romantic connection? Keeping a daily journal can be part of identifying your patterns and the re-occurring life issues. Feedback from friends or a support group can be helpful too, and you can also gather good ideas for individual growth that way. Therapy may be the answer for women with deeper problems. In addition, increasing your social circle by making new friends and getting involved in different activities will help you grow in positive ways.

Ignoring the problem will *not* heal your sore feet. It has to be dealt with. The only question is: *Will you do it?* The quality of your next pair of shoes and your future are asking you to say "Yes!"

Paying for Your Shoes

The cliché *"nothing in life is free"* has validity when it comes to buying your ideal pair of shoes. While you may daydream about the fun you'll have when you get to wear the right pair, it's important to recognize that there will also be a price to pay for them.

This will not be a one-time fee. The price you'll pay will stretch over your entire life together. You'll pay for the shoes daily, whether you want to or not. Of course, the untold rewards of having the ideal shoes can be enormous. That's why a wise choice of shoes is so important.

Money is one way you'll need to pay. Perhaps you were recklessly with your finances in the past. Now you'll need to consider your responsibility to another person when you make your financial decisions. Or maybe you've been extremely careful with your cash. Now you'll need to be open to additional expenditures.

There will be other ways you'll pay for your shoes beyond money matters. Payment will come in various forms, such as sharing your time and space, compromising or trading off on what you want, and weighing the shoes' needs in your decisions. Additional costs will be fewer get-togethers with friends, more need for time management to stay on track with your goals, and the added responsibilities that come from being together. If there are any baby shoes in the household, then multiply the price tenfold.

The idea of paying a price for your shoes can trigger fear. Don't let it scare you. Keep in mind that, with the right shoes, paying will be a pleasure. With each installment, you'll feel more secure in your investment. Paying the monthly fees and watching your investment grow will fill you with joy and pride.

In contrast, if you pick the wrong shoes, paying the price will be very difficult. You'll feel resentful because the return on your investment is will be so low. The exchange will not be even. The price will be high for the little bit that you get back.

Even with the right shoes, there will be periods when the price is more difficult to pay than at other times. What will sustain you is knowing that, over the long term, this is a wise investment. You'll stay and pay because there will be an inner knowing that your relationship with the shoes will improve.

There are few areas in life where the stakes are so high. Choosing the ideal pair of shoes is no place to gamble. You want a sound investment. You're seeking a return on your investment that keeps on giving back. When it comes to selecting your ideal pair of shoes, shop smart. Buying the right shoes will be so rewarding.

Shoe Fit Tip#17: Sometimes while shopping, you'll recognize that the price you'd have to pay for a particular pair of shoes is going to be too high over the long run. It may be difficult to pass up on buying the shoes because of their short-term benefits. You may even be playing that song, "I Can't Live If Living Is Without You," in your head. Cut the drama! You **will** survive and be better off for it. At those times, you'll need to take a step back and look at the shoes realistically. Can you really afford them? Take care of yourself by answering that question honestly. If the price is

out of your range, you'll thank yourself later
when you spend comfortably within your budget
for the right shoes.

Shoes for a Mother's Feet: Special Considerations

Shopping for your ideal shoes can be difficult enough. Want a real challenge? Add children to the picture.

Single motherhood is indescribably difficult without the outside distraction of shopping for shoes. Are you up for pulling off this balancing act? While you might be looking for additional support from the shoes, initially shopping may make juggling everything more difficult. The reality is that you'll need to take time from your children in order to find evenings when you can get away to shop. Do you want to keep all of these balls in the air right now, or do you need to work a few things out before you go to the mall?

If you decide to venture out to shop, what will your guidelines be? Being a parent I know that the most important thing to my wife Theresa and me is to raise children who will become good, productive people. If this is the goal for your children as well, you'll want to pick a pair of shoes that can serve as a good role model for your children. It's also wise to determine if the shoes share your value system. And, at the point in shopping when the shoes and children make contact, notice how well they get along. Are the shoes making an effort to encourage the children to feel comfortable in their presence? In addition, is this pair of shoes hardworking? There will be no shortage of work to do in a blended family. Are the shoes willing to take on some of the financial responsibilities for the children?

Do you find these shoes to be patient and kind? There will be a lot of adjustments to make when the shoes become part of your household. The children will need time to get used to the shoes being around. The shoes will be taking in the reality of day-to-day life with your children in the mix.

Will the shoes understand the demands that your kids legitimately make on your time? If the shoes bring little ones of their own, the children from both sides will have to find a way to get along.

It's possible to find your ideal shoes when you have children, but it will take an exceptional pair of shoes to make all of this work. While shopping, see the shoes you consider in a realistic light. And know that not all shoes that like shoppers with kids are well intended. Remember the self-centered Will character from the film *About a Boy* who pretended to be a dad so he could meet sexy single moms?

Shoes with Children

A single woman may find shoes she likes and later discover they have children of their own. It's important to consider your real willingness to take on the responsibilities that come with this situation. Even if the children only visit the shoes every other weekend, you'll still be entering a family with a history together that existed long before you came along. Let's say a weekend visit goes well with you there; will you understand if the shoes are distracted the following week with family matters? How will you feel about the shoes visiting the mother's home to pick up the kids? Or about the phone calls the shoes and their Ex make to each other to discuss issues involving the children? How about those times when the shoes attend family events without you? Are you willing to work at making the relationships with the shoes' children go as smoothly as possible?

If your time is very organized with few disruptions, buying a pair of shoes with children can totally change your life. Certainly you'll be taking on more responsibility than if the shoes were childless. The time to decide that you're not game for shoes with kids is in the very early stages or even before you leave for the mall. Don't wait until there's an emotional involvement with the shoes and the children.

Shoe Fit Tip #18: When children will be included in the life you'll have with a pair of shoes, consider your choice even more carefully.

While blended families have become the most common type of family in the United States today, few couples in this situation realize what they'll be facing. The bond between you and the shoes will have to be extra strong in order to deal successfully with the complications a blended family can create. Be sure to spend time alone with your shoes to strengthen your connection.

Both Theresa and I brought children into our marriage and we had two more together. The fact that we were both parents at the start helped us understand each other better. I can tell you from my own experience that a top quality to look for in a pair of shoes when you're going to have a blended family is a sense of humor!

Cleaning Out Your Closet

One task that must be done before you buy your ideal shoes and bring them home is cleaning out your closet. You'll need a prominent place in the closet to keep the shoes, so you have to get rid of the clutter. This means you'll need to discard any old shoes that could be competition for your new ones.

It's not fair to your new shoes to just push some old ones to the back of your closet to keep them handy "just in case." When the going gets rough with your new shoes, it will be too easy to go have a fun talk with an old pair of shoes to make yourself feel better. Certainly having such an ego-boosting chat will be a lot easier than dealing with the thorny issue that's come up with the new shoes, however if you don't deal with the relationship problems that surface, they will begin to build a distance between you and the new shoes.

Here are some common ways that we justify keeping old shoes around:

🥿 **These old shoes don't mean anything to me.** I'm just not ready to throw them out of my life yet.

🥿 **What if this relationship doesn't work out?** I'll be very thankful that I still have the old shoes around to pull out again.

🥿 **My ideal shoes should trust me.** It's obvious that I'm making a commitment to them through this purchase.

If you're thinking of holding on to an old pair of shoes, look at your real motivation. Somewhere in the recesses of your mind, do you think that you need a backup plan? Maybe you need to be surer of the new relationship before you make the purchase. Or is it just that you've been putting off the job of cutting that old tie to the other shoes? The time is now if you're ready to make this new commitment.

Is there one particular pair of shoes that is most difficult to give up? Have you never worked through your feelings for these shoes? Think about why you broke off the relationship with them. Are you still somewhat tempted to try them on again? Or is it just nice to keep the fantasy going about what the two of you could be together some day? Now that you're about to embark on a new shoe relationship, weigh your feelings for this old pair. The odds are that you're not seriously thinking of going back to them, but your strong feelings show that it's important to let these old shoes go.

It can be helpful to look at cleaning out your closet from the new shoes' point of view. How would you feel about the shoes keeping contact with another pair of feet that they had feelings for? Wouldn't it be somewhat threatening and confusing? Can you see how a clean break would be more likely to build trust in your relationship, as it would be a sign of the shoes' commitment to you?

It may take a little effort to get that closet cleaned out, but you'll thank yourself after. You will have made a clean break with the past. Also, your new shoes will feel respected and appreciated. If these new shoes truly are your ideal pair, there will be no need to have the old shoes around.

Shoe Fit Tip #19: Sometimes when there's an old pair of shoes available, we turn to them to fill in for areas where our new relationship is weak. Let's say your old shoes are better about talking about feelings than your new pair. So you call up the old shoes to chat when you need a sympathetic ear. The problem is that you're not making the effort to help your new shoes grow. This can undermine your relationship with the new shoes, while strengthening your tie to the old pair. That isn't what you want! In this scenario, it would be better to foster better communication in the new relationship, even if it requires attending couples workshops on the subject or going to therapy together.

Of course, there are some Ex-shoes that we have to keep in our lives, such as the mothers or fathers of our children. Be sensitive to the feelings of your new shoes when dealing with such an Ex. While you don't want to rely more on the old relationship than is necessary, you should be there for your children. Work on keeping a cordial relationship with the Ex so you can provide any support the children will need as a comfortable team. At the same time, stay alert for situations that may trigger sensitivities on anyone's part.

What Type of Shoes Are You Looking For?

Have you been unsure about what to look for in a pair of shoes? Did you believe in "love at first sight"—that you'd just know when a pair was right? Or maybe you did scribble down some sort of Shopping List before you bought this book, but it wasn't very seriously considered. Or when an interesting pair of shoes appeared on the scene, you overlooked what you knew to be crucial criteria on your list? A good pair of shoes is hard to find after all, right?

To bring out the value of a carefully drafted and well-utilized Shopping List, let's compare looking for your ideal shoes to another process. What if you were planning the dream vacation of your lifetime? Let's say it's your one opportunity to go to a destination that has topped your trip list for years. Wouldn't you read up on the sights to see and the fun things to do there? Compare your various options in traveling to and from the destination? Look at how you're going to budget your money to get the most out of this dream trip? Wouldn't there be some places that you'd just have to see in order to feel satisfied with your vacation? Likewise with your love life, you'll have a smoother and more enjoyable time if you give plenty of thought to what you're seeking from your journey.

Here's another example of the benefit of knowing what you want. Can you remember a time when a friend or relative asked you what they should buy you for a gift and you knew just what to say? And, as you opened the gift, your heart was pounding because you had that good feeling that it would be just right. This gift wasn't white socks from Aunt Bess or a tray to make ice cubes in the shape of frogs, but that dream item you were seeking. Wasn't that better than saying they could buy you anything and then ending up with some odd gift not to your liking?

Having a plan to find your ideal pair of shoes may sound unromantic to some readers. Taking a Shopping List seriously and creating it carefully might just seem like too much work. You're a busy gal, aren't you? Well, the rewards for your efforts will start with finding shoes that truly fit your feet and discovering how wonderful they feel. And the rewards will continue as you build a wonderful life that works with your ideal shoes. Plus working on your Shopping List now will save you time that you may have wasted with a pair of wrong, hurtful shoes.

Take a moment to think about your friends. How many of them seem to be just making do with whatever shoes showed up in their lives? Do they complain but keep trudging along anyway in pain? Can you see that if these friends had started out with a well-thought-out strategy and had stuck with it, their lives would be very different today?

The wise approach is to educate yourself about what you want from an ideal pair of shoes **before** you go shopping. Through this process, you'll learn about yourself and have insights that will help bring joy and satisfaction into your life. Your list may even surprise you. It's certainly going to make you more excited about your trips to the mall!

Shoe Fit Tip #20: Romantic notions sometimes keep us in relationships that we know aren't right for us. A handwritten or typed Shopping List will keep your criteria at hand for those times when your hormones or feelings are confusing you about what's in your better interests. Reviewing the Shopping List will help you step back to get a clearer sense of how the shoes really are fitting. The list will be a reality check against any tendency to make excuses for a bad-fit pair of shoes.

On the other hand, the Shopping List can help you slow down to take a closer look at shoes you may have overlooked earlier. If in the past you've gone for flashy shoes that turn out to be a poor fit later, you'll begin to see shoe qualities now that have more staying power. For instance, the right fit in values and goals may start to look more attractive than the best looking shoes in the store. Perhaps the Shopping List in *Men Are Like a Pair of Shoes* will help you answer the question, "What are those qualities in a shoe that make a real difference?"

Creating Your Shopping List

The time has come to compose a Shopping List for your ideal shoes. Think of this Shopping List as being like the grocery list you prepare before going to the supermarket.

What happens when you don't have a grocery list? Don't you find yourself buying some weird supermarket items that you never use and end up throwing away? Also, you tend to spend more money because what you're buying hasn't been well thought out. And if you prepare the grocery list but leave it on the kitchen table at home, aren't there always a couple of crucial items that slip your mind? Sometimes one of the forgotten items is the very thing that prompted you to write the list in the first place!

The purpose of this section is to help you do a thorough job of thinking through what you want in a pair of shoes. Like with a grocery list, your Shopping List will make what you want to buy clear. You won't be wasting time pursuing shoe relationships that don't make sense for you. And your crucial criteria will be at the top of your mind. After reading and using the ideas offered here, you'll have a great Shopping List that you can then fine-tune while you're out and about looking for your shoes.

My List Experience

I learned about making a list of what I was looking for in a mate after going through two painful divorces. My list helped me to find my wife Theresa and we've been happily married now for 13 years. The idea of making a list was originally suggested to me by a friend. This friend told me that she believed I didn't know what I was looking for in a spouse. This made sense to me.

I started my list by jotting down mainly physical characteristics. Most of the original points were the exact opposite of what my ex-wives had to offer with the exception of being Catholic. (Both of my ex-wives had been Catholic.) Note: For your own list, remember that it's important for your items to be stated in a positive way. My first list included:

✒ **Height over 5' 5"**

✒ **Weight appropriate to her height**

✒ **Age – younger than I was**

✒ **Catholic**

As you can see, I wasn't very specific at the start. I believe that, as a result, I didn't date very much right away. However this simple beginning opened my eyes to more things that were important to me. For instance, I realized that I didn't just want a woman who was Catholic; I was looking for a gal who was a *practicing* Catholic. (Neither of my ex-wives had been practicing Catholics.) After years of attending mass alone, I wanted to share this experience with someone.

I also discovered that I wanted to look for a woman who was at a similar stage of growth in her life. I was working on myself and I preferred a partner who could appreciate this and explore the personal growth process with me.

Over time, my list grew longer. I began to date more and the women were closer to what would work for me. At this point, I added a crucial factor to my list: I was looking for *that woman who I couldn't live without*. While I might have married one of various other women that I dated and ended up with an OK marriage, none of them had this special quality until Theresa. Basically what this statement meant to me was that my life would be brought to a higher level by having this special woman as my wife. Including this factor has been important in my marriage; it has sustained me during the challenges that Theresa and I have faced as a couple.

Soon after adding that last point, I read about a support group for divorced Catholics that met weekly at a church in the next town. It was through attending this support group that I met Theresa. She and I were both members of the group for over four months before I asked her out. During our first date, I saw how well Theresa matched my list. We continued dating and got married two months later.

I have been in both unsuccessful marriages and a successful marriage. I can definitely tell you that a successful marriage is much better! So take some time now to think through what will work for you regarding a relationship. The quality of your life will greatly benefit!

This Is Not a Test!

There is no one Shopping List that is correct for everyone. *This is not a test!* You are not required to put any specific trait or factor on your list. Creating a Shopping List is simply a practice that will help the right shoes enter your life. The Shopping List you create will be yours and yours alone. So personalize it. Make it fit *you*.

To avoid a miserable match with your shoes,

think through what you need in a relationship. (Note: Using your computer for this process will make it easier to move items around.) As you saw in my example, it can helpful to:

1. Begin with a list of those traits and factors that didn't work or you didn't like in your past relationships.

2. Turn these items around, and write down their opposite to begin creating your Shopping List. In other words, state the points in a positive way. (For example, if your last shoes were financially irresponsible, note that you're now looking for shoes that are savvy about money matters.)

Now let's go further with the list....

3. Add traits and factors that previous shoes had which were helpful.

4. Expand your Shopping List by reviewing the questions on the following pages. You'll then have the rough draft of your list. (To clarify your perspective on a point, write about it in a journal.)

5. **Your 3-5 Must Haves:** To fine-tune the list, select three to five points that must come with the shoes. These are the items that are absolutely necessary for a relationship to work for you. Making this selection can help you get off the treadmill of bad relationships, if that's been a problem for you. Or it will just help you get what you want now.

6. **Your 3-5 Deal Killers:** Up to this point, you've

stated your overall Shopping List in a positive way. Now you're going to allow yourself to note three to five points that will stop you dead in your tracks if you notice them in the shoes. There is no way that you will accept these factors in a relationship! A "Deal Killer" for me was if a woman didn't belong to the Catholic Church. This doesn't mean that your shoes have to be Catholic or that religion must be even a factor on *your* list. However, *for me*, this was a "make it or break it" item. A Deal Killer for you might be substance abuse, not wanting children, smoking, lack of ambition, flirtatiousness, dishonesty, poor communication skills, etc.

7. **Your Top 12:** Now prioritize the remaining items on your Shopping List. Pick a dozen points that are most important to you.

Your 3-5 Must Haves, 3-5 Deal Killers and Top 12 make up the basic Shopping List. Any remaining items can be referred to as clarifying points when other issues arise. But these three groups will make up the main criteria you'll use to shop.

Very good! Your first Shopping List is complete!

Not Cast in Concrete

As you shop, you'll want to look at your Shopping List as a work-in-progress. You're likely to see that your shopping excursions will help you refine the list over time. You'll also discover that some points aren't as critical as you thought, whereas others that you missed are essential. As you get more experience shopping, simply drop some items and replace them with others.

The Shopping List isn't cast in concrete. Edit the list to reflect what you learn along the Road of Dating regarding your criteria for an ideal mate.

Questions to Ponder Regarding Your Shopping Options

Career

What level of success would your optimal shoes have? Is there a range?

Any type of profession/work you prefer him to have?

If you're working, would his job be similar or different than yours?

What income level would be desirable? Acceptable?

How ambitious do you want your shoes to be?

How many hours would your ideal shoes spend at work a week?

Would you mind a student? Someone who is retired?

Education

How much education would you like your shoes to have? *Any* specific type of degree?
What would feel compatible to your level of education?

Money & Finance

Would your ideal shoes own a home or condo?
Do you anticipate that you both would work?
Do you want him to earn more than you? Do you want your salaries to be at the same level?
Would you care if you earned more?
Do you want to be supported?
If you want or have children, are you looking for someone who could support a family on his income? With both your incomes combined?
Would you mind supporting him? And children?
Would you manage the household finances together? If not, who would be in charge?
Would you have a joint checking account?
Do you expect your shoes to have investments?
How much debt do you think is acceptable?
Where would your ideal shoes stand on the issue of spending versus saving?

Physical Appearance

Are there any physical traits that you'd prefer in your shoes?
Could your shoes be overweight, or thin? Or must

they be "just right"?
Do you have any height requirements?
How intense would the chemistry be with your
ideal shoes?
Is it important that your shoes dress in any certain
way?

Intelligence

Should you and your shoes be at the same level of
intelligence?
Do you want smarter shoes?
Shoes less intellectually challenging?

Values

Traditional vs. Offbeat
Do you prefer traditional shoes or shoes that are
more unconventional?

Religion & Spirituality
Is a religious preference important to you?
If not, would you want someone spiritual?
Is there any type of services that you'd like the
shoes to be open to attending?
Do you want them to already be attending these
services?

Family
Are you looking for shoes that want to raise a family?

If so, how many children?

Would it be OK if he already had children? What age?
How involved would your ideal shoes be with his children?

Are you looking for shoes that don't want a family?
What would his stance be if you got pregnant unexpectedly?

Would you take measures to absolutely prevent this?

Do you want to find someone with strong ties to their own family?

If so, do you want to become close to his family?
Should he be interested in becoming close to your family?

How soon would he want a family if you married?
How would he approach disciplining the children?
Should he be OK with you not working and staying home with the children?

Want to stay home with them himself?

Politics

Do you want him to belong to a particular political party?

Is it OK if his political views are different than yours?

Would you enjoy shoes that liked to debate the issues of the day?

Would you prefer nonpolitical shoes?

Morals

Are there moral issues that you'd want the shoes to

feel strongly about?
Would you reject shoes that told you that they had
been unfaithful before?

Doing His Part
In what ways might your shoes be contributing to
the world?

Sexuality
How much emphasis would your ideal shoes put
on your sexual relationship?
What activities or expectations on his part would
be Deal Killers?
Which turn-ons of yours would you want him to
respect or enjoy?

Lifestyle

Work/Leisure Time
How would your ideal shoes balance work and
leisure time?

Hobbies
Are there any hobbies that you'd want him to
share with you?

Personal Growth
Would it be important for him to be working on

himself?

What would be the optimal ways for him to be pursuing personal growth?

How much of this would you want him to share with you?

Should he be open to participating in any type of personal growth activities with you?

Health & Fitness

How physically active would he be?

Any particular activities he'd be involved with? That you'd share?

How fit would your ideal shoes expect you to be?

How would he approach his diet?

Any particular food preferences (ex. vegetarian)?

Any particular approach to healthcare that's preferable on his part (traditional vs. alternative, or a combination)?

How healthy would your ideal shoes be?

Does he need to be tolerant of any health condition that you have?

Time Together/Apart

How much time would your optimal shoes want to spend with you while dating?

How soon would he want to live with you?

When living together, how many evenings would he want to spend with you?

Spend separately?

Interest in Sports

Would your ideal shoes be a sports buff?
How much time would he spend watching games, matches, etc.?
Would he want to share this with you?
Want you to give him his space?
Do you prefer shoes that are disinterested in sports?

Drugs & Alcohol

Would you prefer that your shoes didn't use recreational drugs?
Is there any use that is OK with you?
How much drinking would be OK with you?
Would you prefer that your shoes didn't drink any alcohol at all?
How would your ideal shoes feel about your use of alcohol or recreational drugs?

Household Responsibilities

How would your ideal shoes want to deal with the household chores like cooking, laundry, and cleaning of the house?
Would he be OK with the idea of having help (i.e. a cleaning lady visiting once a week)?
Would he share responsibility for caring for the children?
Would it be OK if he felt childcare is your job?
Would you want shoes that could take on the

major part of the childcare duties?

Personal Traits

Introverted vs. Extroverted
Would you prefer shoes that were the life of the party or more reserve
Would he like to go out a lot or spend more time at home?
How socially active would your ideal shoes be with others?

Sense of Humor
Should your shoes know how to make you laugh?
What type of humor would he find offensive?

Honesty
How honest would your ideal shoes be?
Under what conditions would it be OK for him to lie, if any?

Trustworthiness
How would your optimal shoes show you that you could trust them?

Optimist vs. Pessimist
Do you prefer a positive thinker or a jaded cynic?
Someone balanced between these two attitudes?

Supportiveness
In what ways would you want support from him?

Emotional Health
How would your optimal shoes deal with challenges?
Should your shoes be skilled at working at differences between you?
Willing to work at this?

Neat vs. Messy
Should your shoes be very neat or more tolerant of messiness?

Talkative vs. Quiet
Do you like a chatterbox or quieter shoes?
Someone in between?

Playful vs. Serious
Do you prefer someone spontaneous and playful, or more structured and disciplined?

Cultured vs. Down-home
Would your ideal shoes be more "high society" or more "just plain folk"?

Intense vs. Laidback
Do you want shoes with a strong personality or someone mellow?

Vital Statistics

What age range would your ideal shoes fit into?
What races or ethnicities are you considering?

Recreational Interests

What types of movies would your ideal shoes like?
What kind of music?
How much TV would the shoes watch?
What social activities would he want to share?
What types of restaurants would he like?

Wearing Comfortable Shoes vs. Finding the Ideal Pair

The experience of shopping for your ideal shoes may feel a bit like an emotional roller coaster. When you think you may have found the right shoes, you'll have feelings of euphoria and excitement. If time shows you that this choice was close but not "it," you'll experience disappointment and sadness. When you're ready to shop again and then locate a pair even better suited for you, you'll be thrilled at the thought of perhaps having picked a lasting pair of shoes.

When you're ready to shop for your ideal shoes, as outlined in your Shopping List, you'll no longer simply be looking for a comfortable pair.

Yes, comfort in the present time is important, but you'll also want shoes that will be able to grow with you over the years. It may take a lot of quiet time and reflection to determine that a pair of shoes is comfortable but not ideal. This is part of the selection process, and you should not feel compelled to stay with shoes that are not a good match. With a well-considered Shopping List, your choices should not be too far off the mark. Yet you may still pick out a few somewhat comfortable pairs before you find the ones with the ideal fit. It will be easier on you both if you don't spend a lot more time with a pair of shoes once you've determined that they don't really suit you.

What's at stake if you linger with a pair of shoes that is simply comfortable rather than ideal? Maybe not a lot, except some of your time. Maybe quite a bit, namely your future with the ideal pair of shoes!

It can be difficult to let go of shoes that feel right in many ways but are missing some crucial qualities. It must be done eventually, however, in order to create the room in your life for the ideal pair of shoes. Sooner is usually better than later. At these times, you must trust your instincts and the process, and know there are plenty of other shoes out there! Focusing on what life could be like with the ideal shoes will help give you the motivation to keep moving forward.

PART IV

NOW WE'RE
SHOPPING
WITH A
SMART HEART!

What We Have Learned So Far about Shoe Shopping

Doesn't it feel great to be so well prepared for your next shopping excursion? Clarifying what you want and need is a key step to bringing it into your life. Now you're ready to apply all that thinking and put it into action.

Somewhere out there, your shoes are thinking of you and hoping to meet you soon. Don't let another pair of feet grab *your* shoes first because you were slow to leave the safety and comfort of your living room! Also, by staying committed to the shopping process described in this book and forging ahead, you'll avoid a fight in the store aisle over shoes that are all flash and no substance. Instead, you'll be shopping smart.

Selecting your ideal shoes will be one of the most crucial decisions you'll ever make. So let's take a moment now to review what you've discovered about the process of shopping for your ideal shoes:

This is a purchase that deserves your careful consideration.

Thinking about men as a pair of shoes will help you make more productive decisions about your relationships with the opposite sex.

In order to successful at shoe shopping, you need to know what you're looking for. This is what creating a Shopping List is all about.

When you're ready for that lasting relationship, you want to shop for a pair of durable shoes—not just ones that will do for today.

If you've had trouble making shoe relationships stick you need to re-evaluate your selection patterns and how you relate.

Hanging onto the wrong shoe relationship because you hope it will change prevents the right shoes from entering your life.

If you've been avoiding shopping, you need to consider what's been keeping you in a holding pattern.

It is OK (in fact it's important) to take time to mend after you end a shoe relationship.

Improving the quality of your life will help you attract better-quality shoes.

If you want emotionally healthy shoes, you've got to make sure you are the right pair of feet to begin with.

Even with a great Shopping List, you may make a few shoe purchases before you find the right ones. (This is explained in further detail in the last section "Wearing Comfortable Shoes vs. Finding the Ideal Pair.") However, the shoes you pick should be very close to being what you want. Don't linger too long with the wrong shoes and keep looking. Revise your Shopping List and reflect on your new observations.

OK, now that you've done the work, you'll know what you want. So where should you shop?

To consider this question, turn to the next section, "Which Stores Are Right for You?"

Which Stores Are Right for You?

The right stores for shopping for your ideal pair of shoes are the ones that sell the type you want. There are really no wrong stores; there are only the wrong stores for the kind of shoes you're looking for. For instance, it would do you no good to shop in a sporting goods store, which sells athletic shoes, if you really want a pair of high heel pumps.

What qualities are you seeking in a pair of shoes? Those readers who worked on developing a Shopping List with the help of Part III already know. If this doesn't include you, go back to "Creating Your Shopping List" and do your homework now. For if you do choose footwear without a game plan, you're setting yourself up for a possible shoe disaster.

One way to start using your Shopping List is to compare it to the inventory of possible stores

I've included below. (Go ahead; take a quick peek.) For easy revision and updating, I suggest you use a computer and tally your "go" and "no go" choices.

Where Do You Want to Shop?

Talk Shops
Church-sponsored raps (This is how I met Theresa.)
Other drop-in discussion groups (Parents without Partners, etc.)
Toastmasters (where people speechmaking)
Weekly mixed gender support groups that you commit to attending

Sporty Stores
Tennis courts or clubs (playing or observing)
Bicycling clubs
Golf courses or driving ranges(to golf or visit during tournaments)
Sports games (baseball, basketball or football)
Sailing clubs
State parks (hiking clubs or park-sponsored walk)
Swim club or local Y's pool
Dances or dance classes
The gym
Sporting goods shops
"Walk-a-thon's or "Runs for a Cause"
Ski Clubs and resorts
Classy Stores
Charity fund-raisers
Symphony or chamber orchestra performances

Country clubs
Wine and cheese tasting

Shop While You Shop or Multi-tasking
Bookstores (including discussion groups and author lectures)
Grocery stores
Men's clothing stores or departments
Record stores
Camera shops
Car dealerships
Computer stores
Hardware stores
Auto part stores
Magazine stands

Heavenly Stores
Churches
Temples and other houses of worship
Choirs (become a member)
Workshops sponsored by religious organizations

Stores for the Health Conscious Shopper
Health food stores
Day spas
Nearby retreats with mineral baths
The waiting room of your massage therapist, chiropractor or nutritionist

Stores with Culture
Museums and art galleries (particularly during openings of shows)

Outdoor concerts
Theatres for plays or musicals
Movies reflecting the shoe's taste (esp. films with long waiting lines)
Comedy clubs

Smart Shops
Adult learning centers
Night classes at colleges
Specialty educators (investing, languages, etc.)
Political rallies or meetings of social groups
Seminars you lead

Stores for Hanging Out
Coffeehouses
Libraries
City parks
Beaches
Restaurants (go alone with a fun book; sit outside on a sunny day)
Food courts
Laundromats
Zoos

Not "All Business" Shops
At your job (select shoes in a different department; be discreet)
Trade shows
Rotary mixers
Professional organizations (volunteer for a committee)
Elevators in office buildings

Moonlight at a job with a social atmosphere

Shops for the Traveler
Airports
Go on vacation alone or with a group
Tourist agents' offices
Take day trips to nearby attractions or picturesque towns

Event Stores
Weddings (don't pick the groom)
Parties thrown by friends
Food tasting
County fairs
Outdoor crafts shows
Farmers markets
Community street fairs

Shoe Fit Tip #21: Reinvestigating personal interests your ideal shoes would share may be the route to finding your mate. On the other hand, perhaps your tendency to stay with familiar stomping grounds is part of the reason you're still single. Try some new shopping places. To make yourself feel more comfortable, begin thinking about some topics you'd enjoy talking about with someone new. Practice some initial conversations in your head. When you're out in the stores, be open and don't be afraid to say the first words. Sometimes connecting is as easy as smiling and saying, "Hello."

Buying Shoes
Over the Internet

"Wow, what a great idea!" "Using a dating website, I'll get to learn everything there is to know about each pair of shoes without ever having to try them on. What better way to look at as many available pairs of shoes as possible than shopping online?"

Do you know someone who has dated a terrific pair of shoes that they found on the Internet and you want to try this approach? Maybe you've even heard about a lucky pair of feet that ended up happily marrying the shoes they met through a dating website. While there's a chance that you may also be so lucky, it's important to realize that the following scenario could occur instead...

Sue visits a dating site and notices a particular set of shoes that look perfect—just what she's looking for! Sue likes the posted pictures and the details that are shared in the description. Immediately Sue e-mails the shoes, and she's delighted when an online corre-

spondence begins.

Each morning, Sue rushes to check her e-mail to see if the shoes have contacted her. Sue is encouraged by the shoes' frequent e-notes and the incredible rapport that develops. After two or three weeks of e-mails, Sue thinks she's falling in love! Sue is thrilled when the shoes suggest an in-person rendezvous over coffee. A date and time are set.

Sue chatters nonstop with her friends about the upcoming "coffee date" and how wonderful these shoes are. Could this be "the one"? In preparation for the date, Sue splurges on an expensive outfit and a visit to the hairdresser. Sue wants to look flawless for her new pair of shoes.

Finally the day of the coffee date arrives and Sue is consumed with excitement! She is careful to get precise directions to the coffeehouse and eagerly arrives about five minutes early. Sue sits happily in anticipation of finally meeting her perfect match. However, suddenly Sue's smile turns into a frown when an unpleasant set of shoes trudges up to the table. Quickly it becomes clear that this pair is the one she met online!

"Wait!" she thinks, feeling a bit confused. "These are not the shoes I expected! I can barely see any resemblance to the pictures that were posted on the website." And when Sue and the shoes talk further, her initial bad feelings deepen. The "great conversationalist" suddenly has turned into "Mr. O. So Boring." Sue can't believe she was "falling in love" with a pair of shoes that would never have received her serious consideration if encountered in real life!

Unfortunately, it's not uncommon for people to misrepresent themselves on a dating website. Deceptive practices range from posting old or overly flattering pictures, to exaggerating or falsifying good personal qualities, to lying about details like weight and age, and to covering up essential factors like one's marital status. There are even people who have fabricated their entire background (leaving out the spouse and kids, of course) and others who have eventually stalked their e-mail correspondents' offline!

Because it's so easy for anyone to distort the truth about themselves on a website, the Internet is not the first place I'd recommend for searching for your ideal mate. However, since this approach has worked so well for some people and is an increasingly popular option, I'm going to provide some guidelines for safe online shopping.

10 Online Shopping Tips

Tip #1: Have fun with your online contacts, but stay alert for any potential red flags. For instance, are the shoes inconsistent in the details they share about themselves? Are they pushy or mean-spirited?

Tip #2: Although it's tempting, don't give out identifying details initially. This includes your regular e-mail address (use an online dating service that keeps you anonymous), home address, phone numbers, or exact place of work.

Can you imagine the possible havoc a crazy pair of shoes could stir up if they suddenly appeared at your office?

Tip #3: If you're clicking with a particular pair of shoes online, keep reminding yourself that you haven't met them yet. Hold onto your heart; don't get too invested until you've tested out the shoes a while in the real world.

Tip #4: After a couple weeks of e-mails, switch to phone conversations before you get together in person. If you're still feeling cautious, call the shoes instead of giving out your phone number. (You can sign up with a low-cost voice mail service to get your messages.) Then check out the emotional quality of the phone conversations and see if your instincts tell you that this relationship is worth pursuing.

Tip #5: Meet the shoes in a public place, such as a popular coffeehouse. It's a good idea not to locate the meeting at the coffee place where you go on a regular basis, in case you'd rather *not* bump into these shoes again!

Tip #6: Wear or carry identifying items so you can recognize each other. The items could be a particular type of hat, a flower in your hair, or a specific book you'll be carrying. This practice helps you avoid confusion about which shoes are there to meet you. (While not about safety, this point can save you embarrassment!)

Tip #7: Tell some friends or relatives about the time and location of the meeting. When you get home, call to report that you've returned. You could even take a friend to the coffeehouse if you'd feel more comfortable.

Tip #8: Plan a short meeting initially. The time can always be extended if you're having fun, but this allows you to bail out gracefully if need be! If the two of you decide to go elsewhere, drive there alone in your own car and don't risk going to a secluded place.

Tip #9: Ask the shoes questions but don't drill them. Let the "getting to know you" process be a natural part of the conversation. Also, be sure to really listen to their answers. Assess the shoes' character. If the shoes now say that they're not looking for a serious relationship, take them at their word.

Tip #10: If you're enjoying the shoes' company and your instincts are positive, plan a second date. While online daters report that it can take a number of "coffee dates" with different shoes to get to a second date, you may beat the odds and accomplish this sooner. For the second get-together, a "recreational date"—such as going to an art opening, an outdoor free concert, or a local tourist spot like the zoo—can keep the tone of your time together less intense (as opposed to going out for an expensive, Saturday night dinner). If you decide to snack together later, choose a casual, fun restaurant. The main theme here is enjoying yourself while playing it safe. Though your online contact could be "Mr. Right Shoes" he could also be "Mr. Very Wrong." As the saying goes, *"Better safe, than sorry!"*

The Discount Bin
(a.k.a. The Bar Scene)

Karen and her feet friends plan a girl's night out. It feels like ages since Karen and her friends have all been together because their lives have become so hectic. The date is set weeks in advance for dinner together and dancing at a place that has a live band on Saturday nights.

For this occasion, Karen wants to look and feel her best. She's careful to watch her portion size and snacking as the girl's night out approaches. She gets extra rest for a few days before the get-together.

The Saturday night finally arrives. She's spent extra time on her appearance, and she feels gorgeous. A honk signals the arrival of her best friend and the two of them are off to join the others for dinner.

At the restaurant, a full reunion takes place with all five of them present. Glasses of wine are passed around and a toast is made in honor of the special occasion.

As dinner comes to a close, she notices the band setting up and the fact that the number of shoes at the bar has tripled. This place has always been a great spot for meeting shoes and since Karen is single, who knows? She might get lucky. *"I'm tired of being alone,"* Karen thinks to herself as she orders a wine cooler.

The band begins to play, so Karen and her feet friends move to a table closer to the dance floor. She notices a nice-looking pair of shoes and makes eye contact with them. The shoes come over her way and ask Karen to dance, which she agrees to do. After a couple of songs and some small talk, Karen excuses herself and makes her way back to her friends. Karen thinks to herself, "Those shoes were fun and handsome. I'm going to look that pair up later to chat some more."

When Karen arrives back at the table, everyone is laughing and having a great time. Karen sits with them for a while, talking and watching the crowd.

Karen starts thinking about her Shopping List and all the work she's done on choosing the right stores. She remembers that nightclubs and bars weren't among the stores listed in this book and wonders if she should consider them as good places to shop. Suddenly it dawns on her that if she were desperate enough to consider having a one-night stand with any of the shoes in this club that the place would quickly become the discount bin. The hook up would probably just be for one-time sex and that's not what she's looking for. *"It's time in my life to find and build a quality relation-ship,"* she reminds herself.

As the night draws to an end, Karen observes that many shoes and feet have been matched up. She notices that this doesn't include the shoes that she danced with. She locates these shoes and the two of them talk a bit more together. With her Shopping List in mind, she realizes that this pair doesn't meet her standards. Going back to her friends, she thinks about what she would do if these shoes did seem to have the qualities she's looking for.

Karen decides that:

The bar scene is a place where a sexual agenda is a high possibility on the part of the shoes.

If she did meet shoes that seemed to be of a better quality at a nightclub or bar, she would move extra slow and check them out carefully. Karen definitely wouldn't go home with the shoes that first night.

She would make sure that the shoes weren't married or otherwise involved with another pair of feet before she became emotionally involved.

It's a good practice to leave a bar with her feet friends.

There are better stores for shopping for her ideal shoes.

Shoe Fit Tip #22: Certainly not every man in a bar is looking for a one night stand but the chances are higher than other places. Also, the alcohol consumption at bars and clubs tends to dampen one's judgment and weaken self-control so it's wise to drink in moderation. Being in a bar also increases the chances of meeting a problem drinker.

While some people certainly do meet over drinks and then later get married, there are also plenty of stories of misrepresentation in the bar scene (just like on the Internet) The classic example of this is the missing wedding ring. Bottom line: My advice is to try other stores instead and keep the bar scene as a place for just a fun night out. If you do meet a Mr. Maybe there, take it slow and check him out thoroughly.

Tips for Working
with Your Shopping List

Once you get out there and start meeting your potential shoes, how do you put your Shopping List to its best use? Start by feeling confident that, with a terrific list, you're on the right track to creating a shoe relationship that will greatly enhance your life.

But how will you know if the shoes fit the bill?

Getting to Know Your Shoes

It only takes a date or two to determine whether a pair of shoes offers real relationship potential. In fact, spending too much time trying to figure this out can be a way to create relationships that go nowhere. Why? Well, when you start spending more time with a pair of shoes in the dating dance. It's only natural to get emotionally attached and then it becomes more difficult to see the shoes in a realistic light. So you hang in there even when there's no real potential for a long-term future with the shoes.

Because of this risk, your assignment now is to have fun checking out various shoes quickly. You'll be asking questions, getting to know the shoes, and finding out what's important to them. If they don't meet your criteria, you're going to move on. That way, there will be room in your life for shoes that are a great fit for your feet.

On that first date, you can put your Shopping List into action as a 10-step dating dance.

Step #1. Review your Shopping List before going on that initial date. With a review, the image of your ideal shoes will be fresh in your mind during a date. As you look over your list, pay special attention to your Must Haves and Deal Killers.

Step #2. Ask the shoes questions related to your list as a natural part of the date; don't grill him as if he's the plaintiff and you're the prosecuting attorney. For instance, you might ask what his job is like and see if you'd be interested in hearing him talk about it over the long haul. Then you could chat a while about your own work or interests. **Example:** On the first date, one pair of feet learned that the shoes' "sales job" involved marketing industrial garbage bins. That was a Deal Killer for her, as she couldn't see herself as Mrs. Garbage Bins. Note: Some possible questions to use on dates are offered in the upcoming "Questions to Ask as You Shop."

Step #3. Start with the lighter questions and then move on to deeper material. Initially you'll want to notice how comfortable the two of you are around each other and whether the conversation flows easily. If you can see that the connection is not going anywhere early on in the date, you might skip the more serious questions and just try to enjoy the time with the shoes.

Step #4. Tell stories to get his opinion. Some topics are easier to deal with by sharing a story and seeing what the shoes' response is. For instance, you could talk about a great time you had with your nieces and nephews to see if he likes kids or discuss a celebrity's infidelity and check out his reaction to someone being unfaithful.

Step #5: Remember to have a good time. Don't be so serious about getting your information that you take the fun out of dating! Playfully connect with the shoes.

Step #6. Notice how much attention the shoes pay to you. Are the shoes asking you questions about your life? If so, this signals the shoes' interest in you and the probability that he isn't self-centered. If he's not tossing questions in your direction, start volunteering information about yourself, and see if the shoes are responsive. A lack of questions from the shoes and inattentiveness could be red flags that you should pass on this pair.

Step #7. As you talk about your mutual interests mentally note possible outings for a second date. Then see if you want to pursue the relationship. Later, if the date is going well, you can bring up some topics again and mention several activities you'd enjoy.

Step #8. During the date, refer back occasionally in your mind to the Shopping List and see how well the shoes are matching up overall. Example: Another pair of feet met shoes for a qualifying lunch date. At first, she noticed that he had many of the important qualities on her list. Later on, however, the shoes talked about being a single dad with joint custody for young children. She realized that he was a very involved dad. Because she already had teenagers of own and didn't want additional responsibility, she passed on these shoes. This gave both the feet and the shoes an opportunity to meet more promising matches.

Step #9. Review your Shopping List when you get home or the next day. One reason to do this quickly after the date is that the information will be fresh in your mind. Even if it's a "no go" with these shoes, you'll want to think about what you learned. In addition to looking at the Shopping List, consider the after the date questions offered in the section "Questions to Ask as You Shop."

Step #10. Write some notes in your dating journal about the first get-together. It's helpful to have a journal specifically for the purpose of writing about your shoe experiences. Scan the questions offered in both Parts III & IV of this book to prompt your thinking.

If there's any subsequent dates with these shoes, follow a similar process.

Acting on What You Learn

After the first date, you'll probably know a tremendous amount about the shoes you've just spent time with. If you found he was a good match to your Shopping List and already agreed to a second date at the end of the first, your next step is clear. The two of you will be going out again soon.

Or perhaps after the initial date, you know the shoes are a promising candidate and hope that they are interested enough to ask you out again. If you have friends in common, let them know you had a great time on the date and are open to seeing the shoes again.

Alternatively, some feet will want to spend more time thinking about the shoes and what they learned about them. Perhaps there's one quality that bothers you and you're not sure whether the relationship's a good idea. Maybe you decide that the shoes' many other traits would make a second date worthwhile. A second meeting would present a chance to check out your reservations and see if you are over-reacting. **Example:** Mary went out with very successful shoes that shared her interests in swimming for exercise, traveling to Alaska, and her value of making work a life priority. However, he seemed to have an overly critical nature. When the shoes called, she agreed to a second date. While this follow-up date was fun, Mary found that her instincts had been right. This was a very critical pair of shoes.

Now the important point for Mary would be to **not ignore** what she learned. Since she couldn't tolerate much criticism, Mary wisely decided to move on and give herself a chance to meet the right shoes.

Bottom line: Act on what you learn—whether you don't want to make the mistake of passing the right shoes by or you know it's not a good match.

Sitting Across from Your Shoes

I remember the feeling I had during my first date with Theresa. It was as if the woman from my criteria list had suddenly materialized before my eyes! During that first date, I suspected that I was going to want to marry her. Theresa seemed to fit what I had described on **my list** so well. I had to ask myself. *"Is it just that I want to make her the right person? Am I adding more to what's there?"* The second date was just a matter of clarifying whether Theresa was as she appeared to be. Luckily, on that second date, I told myself, *"she's the one I want"*.

To prepare for a moment like this read, "If the Shoes Fit, Wear Them." But first, take a look at "Questions to Ask While You Shop." Plan to revisit these questions often while you're in the dating phase.

Questions to Ask
While You Shop

While you're in shopping mode, questions will help you size up various pairs of shoes—both during and after your dates.

During Your Dates

While you don't want to play games of 20 questions during your shoe dates, you do want to sprinkle questions naturally into your conversations that will help create a clear impression of what each pair of shoes is all about. One way to prepare for this is to study your Shopping List and the questions in Part III and think of related questions or reaction-generating stories that you could present on your dates. Either type your questions and stories into your computer or record them in your journal for future reference. Especially think about the questions and stories related to your Must Haves and Deal Killers.

Below are some additional questions to consider:

Who Is He?

How would you describe your philosophy of life?

If you compared yourself to a character in a movie or book, what character would it be?

What's your favorite emotion?

What makes you mad?

What makes you laugh?

How would you describe your basic attitude toward money?

His Past

What has been your best experience in your life so far?

Your worst experience?

What was life like for you when you were growing up?

Are you more like your father or your mother?

What made you fall in love in the past?

His Direction

What five goals would you like to accomplish in your lifetime?

What does the phrase "a successful life" mean to you?

Daily Life

How do you take care of your health?

How do you cope with stress?

Do you expect the best or the worst?

What would bother you more—an overly neat roommate or a messy one?

Relationships

What friends do you spend the most time with?

What do you think the elements are of a great relationship?

How do you picture your main relationship five years from now?

Fun, Fun, Fun

What's your idea of a great weekend?

If you could hear any musician or band live in concert, who would you pick?

If you won a free trip for two to the destination of your choice, where would you go?

<u>After the Dates</u>

During your post date reviews, the following 18 questions will give you additional clarity about how well the shoes match your criteria. Use them in addition to your Shopping List.

1.   Do the shoes fit the work and financial profile you envisioned for your ideal shoes?

2.   Does he have an adequate amount of education?

3.   Do you find him attractive? Is there the right amount of chemistry?

4.   Do you share values regarding religion/spirituality, family and morals in general?

5.   Are you comfortable with his political perspective?

6.   Do you have a feeling for how sexually compatible you might be?

7.   Would his work schedule combine well with your lifestyle?

8.   Do you share common interests in hobbies and pastimes?

9.   Does he seem to be working enough on his personal development?

10.   Do you share fitness, diet and health goals?

11.   Can he offer you the amount of closeness you'd like in a relationship?

12.   Is his interest in sports compatible with the targeted level?

13.   Are you comfortable with his views on drugs and alcohol?

14.   Are your perspectives on roles regarding housework compatible?

15.   Does his personality offer the right mix of

qualities?

16.   Is he the right age for you?

17.   Would the two of you enjoy the same kind of dating activities?

18.   Does he have that special quality that sets him apart from other shoes?

If the Shoes Fit, Wear Them

Fear is a complex emotion. It can keep us from harming ourselves or prevent us from bringing happiness into our lives. The difficulty is recognizing the true source of our fear as we make decisions.

Why would someone be fearful about bringing pleasure into their life? Usually it's because they are more focused on the possible pain this change would bring than on the pleasure. For instance, maybe you've made a painful shoe choice in the last year or two and so it's difficult to anticipate anything but more distress from your love life now. Though this book can't eliminate the possibility of pain being part of your dating experience, my hope is that reading *Men Are Like a Pair of Shoes* has reduced your risk. Why? Because you've taken the time to think through the dating criteria that's right for you. Now it's time to use these criteria wisely.

Love Is Like a House

Have you ever made a large purchase like a house, and then discovered that it was a terrible mistake? Usually this type of mistake is caused when we haven't considered the purchase carefully enough or we allowed our emotions to play too large a part in the decision. Then we want to kick ourselves because undoing the mistake takes more time than if we had been careful in the first place.

Let's look at the house-buying example more closely. While living in a new house is exciting and usually brings you pleasure, it does have the potential to cause pain. Maybe you drove down a street and noticed a beautiful home. You "fell in love" and bought it without thinking much about your requirements. In that case, the pain of a mismatch between the needs of your house-dwellers and the home would be self-imposed. You would have made a better choice if you had systematically considered the important issues related to your ideal dwelling.

A few of these factors would be:

👠 The price (affordable)

👠 Overall size (best for the money)

👠 Number of bedrooms (ditto)

👠 Number of bathrooms (ditto)

👠 Size of the kitchen (ditto)

👠 Present condition/any need for refurbishment (varies)

👠 Safety of the neighborhood (good)

👠 Proximity to shops and services (near)

👠 Quality of nearby schools (high)

👠 (fill in the blank)

This list could go on and on. The longer and more detailed your factor list was, the less likely your chance of making a bad decision. This doesn't mean you couldn't modify a few items on the list to accommodate what's on the market. Also, you may notice something at a particular house that works well for you and want add it to the list.

In this way, buying a house is like loving. Now that you've worked through the Shopping

List process in *Men Are Like a Pair of Shoes,* you shouldn't be making the mistake of not having good criteria for your romantic partner. However, you may still run into some stumbling blocks.

- If you are fearful about connecting with the right shoes you could prolong the assessment phase and painfully prevent pleasure from entering your life.

- If you're a stickler about every item on your list, you may never buy any shoes because the ones you want won't seem to exist.

As you can see, even if you have a Shopping List that's perfect for you, you could remain in pain. That is, if you're too afraid to allow yourself to move forward.

When your list leads you to great shoes that fit, you're going to need to take a leap of faith and give the relationship a chance. This isn't an endless process. There is a goal (finding your ideal shoes!). When you reach it, notice the fear but say, "yes" anyway.

PART V

MAKING
A GOOD FIT
LAST

Shoe Care

Finding your ideal pair of shoes is a wonderful thing. However, making this purchase doesn't mark the end of the effort you'll have to expend to have a great relationship. Once you've bought the shoes, you'll need to take care of them.

How do you take care of a special pair of shoes? You wouldn't just throw them casually into your closet or under the bed like any other pair of shoes would you? No, you'd give them special attention to make them last.

You would:

◢ Set them apart from your other shoes.

◢ Clean and polish them regularly.

◢ Make any necessary repairs of problems that come from daily wear.

If you treated the shoes exceptionally, you'd be rewarded with:

Longevity: the shoes would last a long time.

Comfort: this pair would stay in good shape and remain comfortable.

Pride: because the shoes would reflect the extra care, you'd feel proud of wearing them.

If you provide excellent care for your ideal shoes, will they reciprocate? They surely will. Shoes are more likely to treat you well if you practice good shoe care. So, in order to have a great relationship with your shoes, make the extra effort.

Shoe Fit Tips Even with bright beginnings, relationships deteriorate when they're not cared for. Here are 15 tips for keeping you and your shoes excited about each other.

Tip #1. Stay connected. Make it a point to have some quiet time together every day.

Tip #2. Make him your confidant. Turn to your partner when you need support.

Tip #3. Keep the romance alive. Plan special times out together, whether it's going to the opening of a play, hearing a live concert, or enjoying a simple hike on your favorite trail followed by a creekside picnic lunch. Also, take trips together.

Tip #4. Have a routine. A regular schedule

allows you to know when you're likely to be together or apart. Your joint routine can include a regular commitment to a shared activity, like racquetball lessons or a weekly swim at the Y.

Tip #5. Learn to communicate. Don't escalate your disagreements. (For advice on dealing with your relationship issues, see the next section "Talk to Your Shoes.")

Tip #6. Have fun. Consciously contribute to keeping your relationship positive. Be playful. Keep your sense of humor. Laugh together.

Tip #7. Agree on who does what at the house. I love to cook, so in our home I do the cooking. I also take care of the landscaping and gardening. Theresa enjoys decorating the house. She likes picking out the décor and doing the painting herself. Create a strategy for divvying up the chores.

Tip #8. Be financially responsible. Nothing contributes to relationship problems more than money trouble. Have a system for working with your finances together.

Tip #9. Stay affectionate. Hold hands. Tell the shoes how wonderful they are. Praise the shoes when they do well. Be gentle when they fail. Offer a back rub. Leave a love note.

Tip #10. Work on keeping extended family

ties harmonious. You both had a life before now and family was probably a part of it. Balance the effort of maintaining those connections with the need for space for your shoe relationship. The two of you come first.

Tip #11. Look great. Don't let attention to your appearance wane as the relationship grows older. Buy a new outfit. Take care of yourself by eating right and getting exercise. Get your sleep.

Tip #12. Give him room. You're both sure to have some separate interests. Happily let him go and you may be surprised by how much it revitalizes your relationship. Also, understand his need for some time alone and see how he responds by giving you needed space too!

Tip #13. Keep your sexual relationship strong. Make time on a regular basis for sex. Try something new. Explore your individual turn-ons.

Tip #14. Ride out the low spots. Every relationship has highs and lows. Cruise through the tougher times knowing the overall value of the relationship in your life.

Tip #15. Encourage each other. Having support at home can go far in helping us deal with the challenges of everyday life.

Since communication is so crucial, I discuss it specifically in the next section "Talk to Your Shoes."

Talk to Your Shoes

Shoe-eze is the language of shoes. It's very similar to the language of feet with one major difference. The shoes' language is very direct. If you have a problem with a pair of shoes, they will often not understand this unless you talk to them in a direct way. *You have to tell the shoes exactly what your problem is and then ask them to help you fix it.*

Years ago, a friend of mine came home from work to find half of his furniture and his wife gone. He was shocked. He never saw it coming. At the time my, friend felt that his wife hadn't even told him that there was a problem. In fact, he still believes that to this day.

Now if we were to ask his ex-wife her opinion she might say that she told him repeatedly that they were having problems, or that he simply never really listened to her or seriously considered what she would say to him. Who would be telling the truth here? *Both of them!* The core issue is that she was talking to him in her language and he didn't understand it. She wasn't speaking Shoe-eze.

Let's look at an example that illustrates the power of directness in fostering understanding between women and men:

Example: Two days earlier, Karen had told her husband Tony that she was pregnant and now she'd like to encourage him to take her out to dinner to celebrate. In a phone conversation during work hours, she asked Tony if he feels like going to their special restaurant that evening. Feeling pressured by an important business meeting he's having the next day, Tony absent-mindedly says, "No, I've really got too much prep work to do tonight for that meeting tomorrow." Now if Karen remained indirect, she might just feel hurt and drop the subject. But let's say Karen chooses to be direct at that point and adds, "The thing is, I'd really like to do something special to celebrate our recent news about the baby." Tony then can realize what the conversation is really about and the couple will be able to make plans to go to the restaurant another night.

Here's a basic six-step process for discussing problems in your shoe relationship:

1. Assess the situation on your own.
2. Go to your shoes and explain what the issue is.
3. Express your feelings about it.
4. Suggest a solution and explore it together or brainstorm other options if necessary. Hear the shoe's side as you discuss possible solutions.
5. If a solution isn't found, tell the shoes what the outcome will be if this problem isn't dealt with. Express this in a non-blaming way.
6. Keep negotiating a solution until you find one that you both like.

Remember that shoes understand shoe-eze. This language is direct. Unless you speak to them in their language, they are very likely to miss your message. Talking around an issue won't work. Hinting about what you want is often a futile exercise.

Most shoes are concerned about how they are treating their feet partners. If there's a problem, they just need to be told what's rubbing you the wrong way or what you need that they're not recognizing. Directness is a key to having a happy life with a pair of shoes.

Shoe Fit Tip #23: Working on communication in a shoe relationship is so vital to keeping it alive and well. In her best-seller *You Just Don't*

Understand: Women and Men in Conversation, lin-
guistics professor Deborah Tannen recognized that
part of the problem guys and gals have in relating to each other is the different language styles
they use; she called this "genderlect." Reading
such books can help you and your partner understand each other better. Attending couples workshops that include dialoguing about relationship
problems can be even better as it gives you actual
practice in talking things out. You can also
observe the communication mistakes and skills
that the other couples have.

Keep in mind that speaking directly doesn't
mean being honest in a hurtful way. You need to
consider the timing of your talk; notice if the
shoes are tired or upset about a different matter
and whether choosing another moment might be
more productive.

PART VI

TRY IT, YOU'LL LIKE IT!

The Choice Is Yours

Loving well is a choice. By reading *Men Are Like a Pair of Shoes,* you've shown that you're now choosing to increase your chances of having a great relationship. How well you use the information in this book will have a huge impact on how successful you will be in your selection of a mate.

The concept of a Shopping List worked for me and it can work for you too. I remember sitting across from Theresa during our first date. She met each item on my list. Having dated women for years and being divorced twice, it was hard for me to believe that I could finally be sitting across from the woman of my dreams. It was tremendously exciting!

All the mistakes I had made in my previous selections helped me make a better choice in

Theresa as my wife. However, I couldn't have picked her if I had been approaching my selection process in the same old way. So if you're unhappy with the choices you've made in the past, know that you're on the right track now that you've chosen to go about things differently.

The Shopping List is part of that something different. Work with it and the other ideas in this book to create a happier future for yourself and your shoes.

It's time to have some fun and get out there! Grab your list and get busy shopping. When you find your ideal shoes, write to me at Two Ears Publishing to share your success story. I'm looking forward to hearing from you!

Suggested Reading

Men Are from Mars, Women Are from Venus: A Practical Guide for Improving Communication and Getting What You Want in Your Relationships
by John Gray

101 Ways to Flirt: How to Get More Dates and Meet Your Mate
by Susan Rabin and Barbara Lagowski

Fearless Loving: 8 Simple Truths That Will Change the Way You Date, Mate, and Relate
by Rhonda Britten

Ten Stupid Things Women Do to Mess Up their Lives
by Laura C. Schlessinger

Ten Stupid Things Men Do to Mess Up Their Lives
by Laura C. Schlessinger

Ten Stupid Things Couples Do to Mess Up Their Relationships
by Laura C. Schlessinger

The Cherished Self: How to Give Back to Yourself When You're Living a Life that Takes All You've Got
by Michelle Morris Spieker

When I Say No, I Feel Guilty
by Manuel J. Smith

Dating for Dummies
by Joye Browne

Why Men Commit
by Susan Curtin Kelley

What There Is to Love about a Man
by Rachel Snyder

How to Make People Like You in 30 Seconds or Less
by Nicholas Boothman

2002 Questions and Answers for Lovers: Fun,

Romantic & Revealing
by Cindi Haynes and Dale Edwards

Cast Your Net: A Step-by-Step Guide to Finding Your Soulmate on the Internet
by Eric F. Fagan

The Conscious Heart: Seven Soul Choices that Inspire Creative Partnership
by Kathlyn Hendricks and Gay Hendricks

How Can I Get Through to You? Closing the Intimacy Gap between Men and Women
by Terrence Real

Smart Love: Changing Painful Patterns, Choosing Healthy Relationships: A Codependence Recovery Program Based on Relationship Addiction Support Group
by Jody Hayes

Bad Boys: Why We Love Them, How to Live with Them, and When to Leave Them
by Carole Lieberman and Lisa C. Cool

Don't Call that Man: A Survival Guide to Letting Go
by Rhonda Findling

The Conscious Bride: Women Reveal Their True Feelings about Getting Hitched
by Sheryl Nissinan

The Seven Principles for Making Marriage Work
by John M. Gottman and Nan Silver

The New Intimacy: Discovering the Magic at the Heart of Your Differences
by Judith Sherven, Ph.D., and James Sniechowski, Ph.D.

Resources

Advice Websites

www.innerself.com, articles on relationships & personal growth

www.lovingyou.com, extensive site with information on love and romance

www.parent.net, offers free e-newsletter on parenting issues

www.optimalthinking.com, using your mind for more success in relationships and business

Workshops

Jeff Carta: Men Are Like a Pair of Shoes Workshops & Seminars, for info on various topics, such as the mate selection process, getting ready to date, dating smart, etc. More info at www.menarelikeapairofshoes.com.

Life Works, especially for professional women who wonder why they're still single, www.life-worksgroup.com/

Positive Way, seminars on enhancing the quality of your relationships, www.positive-way.com

Support Groups

North American Conference of Separated & Divorced Catholics, www.nacsdc.org/

Parents without Partners, www.parentswithoutpartners.org/

Codependents Anonymous (CODA), support group for people involved with those who abuse addictive substances, www.codependents.org/new-com.html

Internet Dating

www.match.com

www.americansingles.com

www.singleparentmeet.com, for you single moms looking for single dads

www.sportsmatesearch.com, for athletic singles

www.catholicsingles.com, Catholic-oriented

www.jdate.com, Jewish oriented

www.rightstuffdating.com, for singles who graduated from top level colleges/universities

Quick Order Form

Fax orders: 949/454-9862. Send this form.

Web orders: www.menarelikeapairofshoes.com

Postal Orders: Jeff Carta, Two Ears Publishing, P.O. Box 1300, Lake Forest, CA 92609

Please send **FREE** information on (check off your selections):
Other Books !
Author Appearances !
Seminars & Workshop !

Name: _____
Address: _____
City: _____ State: _____ Zip: _____
E-mail Address: _____

Price: $14.95

Sales Tax: Please add 7.75% for products shipped to California addresses.

Shipping

U.S.: $4.00 for first book and $2.00 for each additional book.
International: $10.00 for first book and $5.00 for each additional book.

Payment: Visa _____   Master Card _____
Card number:

_____
Name on Card: _____
Exp. Date: _____